CLUES

THINK POSITIVE, PRACTICE GRATITUDE AND UNCOVER YOUR LIFE PURPOSE

MELISSA BUTTERWORTH

This publication is designed to provide accurate and authoritative information regarding the subject matter covered. It is provided with the understanding that the author and publisher are not engaged in rendering legal, accounting, tax advice, or providing career or life coaching. If legal or tax advice is required, the services of a competent professional should be sought. This book and all the intellectual property rights therein shall at all times remain the exclusive property of Melissa Butterworth.

ISBN: 978-1-7329555-4-7 (paperback)

ISBN: 978-1-7329555-5-4 (hardcover)

ISBN: 978-1-7329555-6-1 (ebook)

Published by Melissa Butterworth

www.TheAmericanInterns.com

This book is for the billions of women on this planet who aspire to reach their full potential. It is my God-given mission to provide each of you with the tools needed to exceed every expectation and fulfill every dream that you have within you. As women, may we learn to encourage and lift one another up, establish the mindset and practices to exceed our wildest dreams, and start to recognize and connect the clues that show us our path forward.

CONTENTS

INTRODUCTION

ARE YOU READY FOR A
LIFE-ALTERING CHANGE?

If you're reading this book, you're ready for a life-altering change. This is no small thing. You're about to create exactly what you set out to create. You set an intention to receive this empowering and educational content because you've likely been curious about life and the universe.

Have you found yourself thinking about or asking the following questions?

- Am I completely satisfied with my life?
- Are there areas of my life I would like to change?
- Is there something I believe I was made to do or be, and I just can't get there?
- Why am I here on this earth?
- How do I know what my life purpose is?
- How do I know what my strengths and talents are?
- Why have I had some challenges and setbacks recently?
- What tools and steps do I need to take to achieve my life purpose?
- How do I start to recognize some of the clues that are present in my life?
- How do I go about creating a road map to achieve my dreams?
- How do I implement this road map?
- Where do I go to find mentors to help me achieve my goals?

- How can I manifest whatever I put my mind to?
- Why do I feel anxious, unsettled, and bored, as if something is missing from my life?

If you've ever asked yourself these questions, you're not alone. According to a survey of 26,000 LinkedIn members conducted by *The Guardian*, 74 percent of respondents want a profession where they feel like their work matters. Most of us are searching for purpose and a deeper meaning in our lives.

You know that the journey of life contains millions of stages, steps, decisions, and impactful events (both expected and unexpected). Unfortunately, life doesn't come with an instruction manual—not even a pamphlet. But you're exactly where you are supposed to be right now, and you have the ability to move forward to where you long to be.

Seventeen years ago, I thought I was living my dream life when I was unexpectedly fired from a job that I loved. I was personally and professionally devastated. I felt stuck and had no idea where to turn, and I am sure many of you can relate to that dreaded feeling. But hope is not lost.

As you work through this book, you'll notice that the terms *stages* and *steps* are used often. That's because there are many different stages of life, and within each stage, there are several steps to take as we move forward toward our goals.

The information in this book will provide the exact tools needed to fulfill all your life dreams. The stories, steps, and stages provided within have been applied, with proven results, by dozens of women who walked many versions of this journey.

What you're about to read are the life stories of some incredibly talented and successful women who turned ideas and thoughts into organized plans. These are everyday women of all ages, ethnicities, and cultures who implemented a proven and tested process and discovered their life purpose. They're sharing their stories for the purposes of your education and encouragement.

I am confident that you'll feel inspired by what you read in the following pages. I am even more confident that after reading this book and implementing its suggestions, you will reach a major turning point in your life.

Being a woman who lives with purpose means getting out of survival mode and being able to sleep soundly at night.

It means contributing to causes that you believe in.

When you find your purpose, the money follows.

This results in wealth for yourself, your friends, and your family. It's important to note that wealth means something different to everyone. It could mean monetary gain, education, trips, or owning a home. But more importantly, living with purpose means discovering what you're passionate about and making that your life's focus, living with the feeling that you're contributing to an important mission in life.

You're about to learn how these women uncovered their life purpose and became powerful, confident, radiant beings of light and love. Outlined in this book are the steps that these women took over the past several decades. It describes what to do and how to do it. It contains a complete guide to uncovering your God-given purpose, along with tried-and-true processes that, when implemented, will ensure you exceed your wildest expectations.

While you may not need all the information provided within this book, just one idea, plan, or suggestion can get you moving toward your goal, potentially making this one of the most important books you will read.

I am an ordinary woman who is living an extraordinary life. And no, it isn't because I went to the best schools or had the best connections, but instead because I took my success and happiness into my own hands. I became self-reliant and started to think like an entrepreneur. Being self-made is an honor and is something that I am grateful for every day. I had a dream along with the desire and discipline to work toward my aspirations, and ultimately I made things happen.

Everybody has a different definition of being self-made. To me, being self-made means taking power into your own hands, becoming your own hero, and creating your own reality. You reach a point where you understand that no one else can do it for you. You are 100 percent responsible for your own success. You become the captain of your own vessel. You determine your own value—not a man, not a boss, not a job or a corporation—YOU. You are in charge and have the ability to reach whatever your dreams may be.

The only person you can change is YOU. When you change yourself and decide to step into your power, the people around you will change because of the radiant aura that emanates from within. You won't need to say anything, because you'll send a message to the world that says, "I am complete."

As a business creator, founder, CEO, and female self-made multimillionaire, I have worked with people from all walks of life. I have helped them make life-altering changes. I've sat with them, experienced their ups and downs, listened to them, encouraged them, cheered them on, and helped them reach their full potential. Mainly, I have helped them become far wealthier than they ever imagined.

The purpose of this book is to empower women of all ages. My dream is to get this book into the hands of every woman. I am passionate about this because I was fortunate to have been raised by parents who taught me that I could become anything that I set my mind to. I have a mother who is extremely driven and has been my lifelong mentor (you'll learn more about her story soon). I have a father who is hardworking and intelligent, who encouraged me to get an education and find a career that I loved.

This book is divided into three sections. The first section is designed to help you understand the big picture and where you currently reside. The second section includes several chapters that discuss important steps that you must take to develop a sustaining lifelong foundation. The third section was designed to help you uncover your strengths, talents, and skills while uncovering events (clues) that are leading you toward your purpose.

Each section consists of scattered clues to assist you in your journey. In the following chapters, you'll learn about and hear directly from dozens of women who started off just like you. Each one of these women mastered the steps that you are about to learn and have successfully become self-made.

YOU WILL BE INTRODUCED TO THE FOLLOWING STEPS ON THIS JOURNEY AS YOU VENTURE THROUGH THIS BOOK:

Step 1:   Understanding Where You Are

Step 2:   Recognize the Power of Your Subconscious Mind

Step 3:   Using the Law of Attraction to Train Your Subconscious Mind

Step 4:   Applying Gratitude to Your Daily Life

Step 5:   Creating a Positive Mindset

Step 6:   Developing Sustaining Self-Confidence

Step 7:   Discover Your Strengths, Talents, Vision, and Purpose

Step 8:   Identifying Clues through Events, People, Places, and Life Experiences

Step 9:   Surrender Your Life Purpose to the Universe

Step 10: Your Magical Future: Returning with the Elixir, and Giving Back

The women in this book and I have personally walked the walk, and we're going to share each and every step that, when applied, will unlock the untapped potential within you. While high school and college teach us valuable lessons in academia, teamwork, discipline, time management, communication, independence, conflict resolution, and so on, there is often an overlooked area that is not taught. While all of the knowledge learned in school is important, what you will read about in this book will become the most critical lesson of them all.

Before we get into the details about *CLUES*, it should be stated that while this book is focused on empowering women, it doesn't mean that men can't benefit from the information. It is simply focused on women because I have personally achieved these goals and want to mentor and help women of all ages. I am a firm believer in helping other women achieve success early on in their journey. I have seen far too many women try to sabotage the success of other women due to jealousy, insecurity, and ambition.

If you get only one message from this book, this is the most significant: **you can and will become whatever story you create for yourself.** That's right—if you want to become a CEO, surgeon, teacher, self-made millionaire, billionaire, or even the first-elected woman president of the United States of America, then, with God's grace and your hard work, that is exactly what you will become.

Background, Themes and Key Definitions
Life as a Treasure Hunt

Life is seldom lived in a straight line. It's full of zigzags, curves, and choices that will change the trajectory of your life. Think of it like a treasure hunt. We'll use this analogy throughout this book. You're hunting all along for clues and answers that point you to your purpose. At the end of the day, you're searching for the X that marks the spot.

It isn't until you've gone through a number of stages, taken a number of steps, and identified the clues along the way that you find the treasure—your answer—has been inside of you all along. You had to go through the process to discover your hidden talents, your purpose, your goals, and your self-confidence. As you learn to master each step of this exciting journey, it's my dream that each one of you finds the key to unlock your own hidden treasure.

The treasure hunt theme was created as part of a marketing contest that I conducted in the spring of 2021 at North Broward Preparatory School in Coconut Creek , Florida. This school was chosen because it had implemented the Learn to Start model for transforming education. This model from The Startup Studio focuses on developing students so that they can learn to start their lives and futures in a way that aligns with who they really are—their passions and their interests.

The Startup Studio is a complete solution that connects education directly to entrepreneurs in the marketplace. Each student has an opportunity to attend an annual three-day symposium where they can pitch their business idea to a panel of entrepreneurs who provide valuable feedback specific to the products and/or services, financial models, and feasibility of the students' ideas.

As a successful entrepreneur and CEO, I was invited to speak to the class in 2021. As a part of the speech, I conducted two contests to encourage the students to think deeply about their own purpose.

Carly Burr, a junior at the time and an eager student enrolled in The Startup Studio program, attended my guest appearance and was ambitious enough to enter both contests. Of the 100 people that had the opportunity to enter, Carly won the marketing theme contest and became the first annual American Intern. This contest tested participants' ability to come up with the best marketing strategy to apply toward this book. As a result of this idea, I awarded her with a paid internship, cash prize, and her treasure hunt marketing theme that she created has been applied to this book. In addition, Carly has contributed to the writing, editing, and development of the book. During this process, she has discovered the clues that have led her to find her life's purpose.

Sabrina Riback, a sophomore at the time and another determined student, also entered both contests and was the winner of the Life Purpose contest. This contest instructed participants to write out one hundred life events and were encouraged to think through the meaning of those events. The goal for this contest was to test the participants' ability to recognize the clues and themes that had shaped their lives. Because of her thorough submission, I awarded Sabrina with a cash prize. Along with this, she also assisted with the writing and editing of this book.

The idea behind the American Intern Program is to continue creating contests on an annual basis for students worldwide and allow winners to be exposed to other successful entrepreneurs. For more information on how you can enter the annual Life Purpose contest and become a future winner of the American Interns, visit www.TheAmericanInterns.com.

The American Interns

The American Interns program was started in the summer of 2021 as a result of my work on this book. Women worldwide will be provided with the opportunity to apply the information presented throughout this book by entering an annual Life Purpose contest similar to the one conducted at Carly and Sabrina's school. Those who choose to enter the contest will be given the opportunity to win cash prizes, an internship, and the chance to be featured on our website. To learn more about the details of this once-in-a-lifetime opportunity, visit our website at www.TheAmericanInterns.com.

Treasure Hunt Rules

Throughout this book, you will be presented with various treasure hunting rules and additional guidance on how to better recognize and follow life's clues. These are general rules of thumb that can be applied in different situations. These rules may invoke different feelings for different readers. As you go through the book, use your own personal journal as you begin to create your own book of clues. You can use this to start writing down your dreams, intuitions, hunches, or feelings. As you write down more clues, you will start seeing the patterns in your life. You will use this journal for the rest of your life, as your road map to all of the great treasures that await you.

Clues

During your personal journey, you'll be provided with many clues along the way. Many of these clues will start to appear as you read this book and perform the exercises. These clues can come in many forms and are dependent on your own life circumstances. Be sure to look carefully as you read each of the following chapters and take note of the clues that have meaning for you.

Each person reading this book possesses their own purpose, passion, and potential. While each of us experiences unique life situations, there is usually a familiar recurring theme that is important to recognize. The clues presented throughout will help solidify an idea and drive home a life lesson meant for you at some point in your life—maybe even at this exact moment. It is important that you participate in the exercises presented in this book, as many of the clues will come from your own experiences. The only way to identify them will be to jump in and do the work.

CLUE

"You can't connect the dots looking forward. You can only connect them looking backward. So you have to trust that the dots will somehow connect in your future. You have to trust in something—your gut, destiny, life, karma, whatever. This approach has never let me down, and it has made all the difference in my life."

—STEVE JOBS

Follow the Clues to Find the Treasure

If only we had the treasure map laid out clearly in front of us, we could follow the clues to find the treasure. What if, because you couldn't see the treasure map all at once, you had to find the clues one by one? What might help would be having a wise mentor to guide you to the people and places that would make a difference in your life. However, once we realize that we all possess our own "internal mentor" who is constantly sending us clues, we begin to see things in a different light. Our challenge will become recognizing the clues and acting on them.

Clue Catchers

Like in any treasure hunt, you will be provided with clues along your life's journey. Your job is to become aware and to start "catching the clues" as they arise. These clues can come in many forms and are unique to you. They may come in the form of gut feelings, visions, places, events, encounters with others, dreams, bodily sensations, or simply hunches. These clues offer us guidance, like a personalized GPS, to keep us on track in the treasure hunt of our lives.

The key is to start recognizing the clues—and *act* on them. These clues almost always involve an internal feeling that is further sparked by some external stimulus. Have you ever caught yourself thinking about someone you haven't heard from in a long time, and then they call you the next day? This is a simple example, yet it teaches us how to recognize and follow the clues in our own lives.

One clue leads to another clue over time. Clues have many stages and, if we are willing to seriously examine them, slowly reveal a larger pattern. Remember, if finding the treasure was easy, there wouldn't be much point in the treasure hunt.

Your book of clues will become the most important book of your life. It will reveal to you, one piece at a time, the treasure map of your life and the work that you're meant to do while you're in it. Your treasure map isn't just about work, of course; it is about recognizing the people who will make an impact on you and pursuing those relationships.

Clue Connectors

There are several goals to aim for as you read this book. One of the single most important goals is to master the art of recognizing clues. Once you recognize the clues, you need to learn how to start connecting them. Throughout the book, I have included some of my own personal clues that have had significant meaning in my life. By the end of the book, my goal is to share how these clues began to connect with one another to lead me to my own treasures.

As you go through this book and complete the exercises, you will identify various clues that resonate with your own life. Some clues will stick and others won't. The key is to take note of those clues that sing to your soul. Take a moment to write them down in a journal that you will carry with you throughout life. You will eventually develop the ability to determine relevant versus irrelevant clues, the meaning of these clues, and how to act on them. It takes time to develop this newly learned skill. Once you do, you can be proud to call yourself a "Clue Connector."

The Golden Key

This book will be unlike any other you've read. You, the reader, will have the opportunity to enter the American Interns annual contest and potentially win the Golden Key. Perhaps you know someone who may benefit from entering and winning this once-in-a-lifetime opportunity. The Life Purpose contest will allow you to apply the information learned throughout this book to assist in uncovering your life purpose. The Golden Key can be used to unlock your own treasure chest that consists of several prizes. The winners will have the opportunity to win cash prizes, participate in a summer internship at a company of one of the women featured in this book, and be featured on our website.

Inspiring Stories

Many chapters include stories from women of all backgrounds, ages, and ethnicities who have agreed to share their real-life experiences to inspire other women. They are stories of past and present events that helped shape who they have become. These are stories of inspiration, integrity, greed, trauma, devastation, despair, and, in some cases, outright stupidity. Some are useful and educational, and some are just plain entertaining. In life, reality is often stranger than fiction.

You'll be introduced to the life journeys of these fascinating women:

- The founder of Orangetheory® Fitness
- The chief lab officer of the largest healthcare corporation in the world
- A retired Dell sales executive (known as a "Dellionaire")
- Entrepreneurs who made millions by starting businesses in extremely niche markets such as laboratory mergers and acquisitions
- A financial estate planner for the mega-rich
- A top mergers and acquisitions (M&A) attorney
- A world-class organizer
- A teacher-education disrupter
- A top urologist
- A hairstylist who created a game-changing hair product
- A fashion designer for the stars
- A reality TV star, actress, influencer, and product developer
- An entrepreneur, housewife, and cancer survivor
- Four students who inspired the creation of The American Interns and current annual Life Purpose contest

Exercises

You will be invited throughout the book to participate in various exercises. Doing the exercises will ensure that you're applying the principles learned throughout this book. It's one thing to learn and another to apply what you've learned. Our goal is to accomplish both.

Epiphany

Have you had enough of your current situation? Do you look around and know that you desire more in life but don't know how to go about obtaining it? Do you sometimes feel as though you're great at identifying what *isn't* working in your life, but are now ready to find what *will* work for you? If you answered yes to any of these questions, you're not alone.

The day may come when you'll wake up and say, "I have had enough." A part of you may feel numb, or maybe even like a member of the walking dead among millions of other human zombies going about the motions of life but not feeling fulfilled. You'll know that something is missing in your life and will have likely looked for happiness through external remedies like friends, movies, or addictions (shopping, food, alcohol, sex, drugs, work, and so on). You'll look in the mirror and not recognize the person staring back. This will be one of the most painful times in your life, and it will seem as if you've lost all hope. You may feel depressed, lonely, angry, scared, mad, frightened, or even a bit desperate. You'll know that something must change. You can do what you've always done and continue getting the same results. Or you can choose a new direction.

This very moment will become the most critical choice in your life. Life is a puzzle that reveals itself slowly. You arrive at a fork in the road, a place where going left or right could change the entire trajectory of your story. Over time, if you're fortunate, you'll look back at these defining moments as the events that showed you who you are and who you could become. It will be at this very moment that you have a major epiphany. The something that must change is *you*, and no matter what you must do to climb out of the dark, dismal hole, you can and will do it.

Once you've consciously made this decision, your life will change forever. It will be then that you'll start the most important journey of your life—the journey toward discovering your life purpose.

EXERCISE
Say Goodbye to the Old You

Take a moment to open a blank journal. It's time to reflect on where you are in the present, be thankful for how far you've come, and give thanks for any recent awakenings that will allow you to move to a higher level of awareness.

Start by giving your old self a nickname that reminds you of someone you appreciate and love but are ready to say goodbye to. For example, perhaps you have a difficult time with procrastination and desire to get certain aspects of your life moving forward. As you think about a possible nickname, you might pick the name of someone who betrayed you, or a name that is unpleasant based on your own experiences with that person.

Gretchen was the name I had given my old self when I first went through this exercise. I used Gretchen because she was someone who had come into my life and didn't have my best interest at heart. She gave me some bad advice and I was too young to understand the consequences of applying that advice.

Look at this exercise as somewhat bittersweet. You're about to say goodbye forever to an old friend, which might make you feel somewhat sad, but you're more excited to embrace the path forward as you embark on all the new experiences ahead. It's important to give yourself grace and not be angry with yourself. After all, you wouldn't be where you are without those experiences.

Write this down in big bold letters and read it to yourself until it resonates deep down in your soul:

> *She looked at her old life one more time, took a deep breath, and whispered, "I will never see you again, [old name]. I am grateful for the experience and am looking forward to becoming my new self and all the incredible versions to come."*

Now it's your turn.

Wake Up to Reality before You Sleep Your Life Away

You won't be able to control what happens to you in life, but you have total control of how you react. That's right, you heard me. Read this again and again until it resonates. You are done with being a victim and ready to move to a higher level. Start today by making changes in your life, especially with how you've been thinking.

Do you currently feel as if something is missing in your life? Are you bored, anxious, or feeling stuck, stagnated, or maybe even numb? The reason is simple. You aren't living your life purpose. The main difference between someone who is thriving professionally, financially, spiritually, emotionally, and romantically and someone who isn't is simple: The thriving person is living their purpose.

If you don't know what your purpose is, or thought you knew and no longer do, that's okay. You are exactly where you're meant to be at this stage in your life. There are no mistakes or coincidences. Everything that happens to you is meant to be. Your purpose will become clear once you apply the tools you're about to learn in this book.

Discovering your life's purpose will be one of the biggest events of your life. Once you do, everything around you will change. Your life will turn around and doors will open. You won't have to chase money; it will suddenly appear. When you bring your purpose to life, you'll suddenly become happy with or without a spouse by your side. If you're meant to marry, your soul mate will suddenly appear along your journey without having to think about it. Your dependence on food or other addictions will subside with intentional work and focus. Your purpose will guide you to the career of your dreams. And, most importantly, you will no longer live as a victim, trapped in the past.

The person you once looked at in the mirror, the one you didn't recognize, will become a distant memory, and you'll finally be set free! Please listen closely: discovering your purpose won't be easy. You are going to have to dig deep and put in some work. It will be much deeper work than you've ever done in the past. That's why you're here, isn't it? Deep down, you've always known that you were meant for something far greater than what you're currently doing.

In order to uncover that purpose, you must be willing to get to work. Let's get started.

PART I

1

LET THE HUNT FOR CLUES BEGIN

Melissa Butterworth
CEO, ENTREPRENEUR

MY FIRST CLUE: FLASHBACK

The smallest thing can change your life. In the blink of an eye, something happens by chance, when you least expect it, and sets you on a course that you never planned, into a future you never imagined. Where will it take you? That's the journey of our lives, our search for the light. But sometimes finding the light means passing through the deepest of darkness. At least, that's how it was for me. The following accident was one of my earlier clues.

1979, Harrisonburg, Virginia

On the last day of third grade, my right arm was severed from my body. I had been playing on a seesaw with a classmate when she decided it would be entertaining to jump off her end while she was on the ground. I did what most kids would do and hung onto the handlebars for dear life. When gravity kicked in, my 5 foot 6 inch, 100-pound body slammed into the concrete with such force that my right elbow tore right through the ulna, lateral epicondyle, radius, and articular capsule. In simple terms, my elbow was shattered. The collision sent my brain into shock. The wave of initial pain was severe. In a fraction of a second, I went from a healthy, happy nine-year-old to a girl in danger of losing her arm, if not her life. Of course, my nine-year-old self had no idea of the severity of my injuries at that moment.

When I managed to get up from the concrete, it was somewhat of an out-of-body experience. While my entire right arm was, in medical terminology, severed from my body, the skin was still holding it together. I somehow managed to lean down, pick up my arm from the concrete, and stumble over to my teacher. By the look on my teacher's face, I knew it wasn't good. She put her arm around me, and we began the long walk to the nurse's office: across the playground, over the hill, up the stairs, and down a very long hallway. I didn't realize that every single minute mattered. Apparently, neither did anyone else.

When we arrived at the nurse's office, the nurse immediately grabbed what was left of my right arm and asked, "Does this hurt?" I was in such shock that I immediately yelled, "Well, what do you think?" (I presume that this is why, to this day, I still use humor and sarcasm in moments of despair.) Looking back, I suspect her reaction was likely due to having never encountered a situation like that before. She then proceeded to ask me a series of questions.

"What year is it?"

I said 1989. (It was actually 1979.)

"What is your mom's name?"

"Uh. Um." Twenty seconds must have passed. I answered with "Mom."

That was the last question I remembered. My body was in shock, and the loss of blood supply from my broken extremity was taking a toll on my brain's ability to think logically. My blood pressure had dropped, and I was dizzy and nauseous. This wasn't the first time, and wouldn't be the last, that I experienced severe anxiety.

To add further shock, the nurse made what could have been a fatal decision: to call my mom. That's right—not 911, not a doctor, but my mom. You would think that she would have used more common sense.

By the time my mom arrived, I must have looked like a ghost, because my mom drove over 100 miles an hour toward medical care. But instead of taking me directly to the hospital, she took me to my pediatrician. The pediatrician took one look at me and my arm and told my mother to get me to the hospital *immediately*. Thank God he did that.

The drive to the hospital is not a memory I can recall. However, once I arrived at the emergency room, I was greeted by a staff of several nurses and doctors, all of whom my pediatrician had called.

I was immediately rushed into emergency surgery.

My parents were no strangers to this hospital. Two years earlier, on one icy, cold Monday morning, my father had entered the same emergency room to see my mom, my brother, and me after we'd been in a bad car accident. My mother and I had been beaten up pretty badly. I only recall two things from that accident. I remember asking my brother, Ed, "Are we in heaven?" I thought we had died. I also asked my mom if the blood stains all over my faux fur coat (which I was wearing for show-and-tell that day) would ruin the coat.

You must understand, fashion has been in my DNA since I was a kid, and that coat meant *everything* to me. My family didn't have the means to buy me much, and this coat was a luxury that I cherished. I seemed more concerned about my coat at that moment than whether we were physically okay. Looking back, it really is quite peculiar what happens to the human brain during traumatic moments.

Luckily, we walked away from the hospital alive and healthy.

Now, after two years of normal life, my parents found themselves back in the same place, with their youngest child facing the possibility of losing her arm and her life.

After several hours of surgery (according to my mother), I remember waking up in a hospital room with my father, in his own hospital bed. I didn't understand why my father was lying next to me, as if he was now a patient.

Had I woken up from a bad dream?

Had I died and was getting a glimpse of heaven? Don't worry. I'll pick up this story soon enough.

CLUE

"It is the light in the lantern that shows you the path, not the lantern."

—ANONYMOUS

Step 1: Understanding Where You Are

It's astounding how life events can change the trajectory of our lives. The accident with my arm would leave more than physical scars. I went from a normal, happy-go-lucky child to a scared, timid, and anxious child. For many years after my accident, I struggled with multiple areas of my life (like most teenagers), including

- My identity
- Anxiety and depression
- My thoughts
- Self-confidence
- Body image
- The influence I allowed others to have over me
- Comments that I told myself repeatedly without being consciously aware
- Comments of others that I allowed to shape my way of thinking
- Who I was supposed to be
- My strengths and values
- My life's purpose
- What truly made me happy
- Being aware of the clues that were put before me to assist in my overall direction in life
- Being in tune with my inner voice
- Understanding why bad things happened to me

Struggling with all of these issues led me on a journey to find answers about the meaning of life, and my role in it. Having my arm severed at such a young age, along with several other defining moments (clues), led me through my own Hero's Journey and brought me to my elixir: sharing my life's purpose through this book. I equate the term *elixir* to having a similar meaning as when we experience an aha moment.

Think of those aha moments that you have experienced at some point in your own journey—those magical moments when everything comes together and anything that seemed questionable suddenly makes sense. It might have been a bad breakup that you went through, only to later meet "the one" at an event you never would have attended had you not gone through the breakup. For me, my experiences with several medical situations ultimately led me to my aha moment or elixir and the discovery of God's calling for my professional life. At the time, I didn't understand why I was going through some of these challenges, but over time they began to make sense.

I didn't have all these awakenings (clues) or aha moments at one specific age and or moment in my life; it's a lifelong process. All my life experiences and ability to interpret these moments have shaped me into the woman that I have become. This will happen for you once you learn to take the clues from these events and turn them into positive defining moments. These events will no longer be viewed as setbacks, but rather setups taking you closer toward your destiny.

I experienced awakenings in my early childhood and in my twenties, thirties, forties, and fifties. After examining my own life events and understanding their deeper meaning for my life's purpose, I am blessed to be able to share my story and inspire others. Even more exciting are all the women's stories that you'll read shortly. They all come from different backgrounds and have overcome their own trials and tribulations. They are walking inspirations. Each one of them has learned and applied the tools within this book and has found her own internal hero. If we can do it, you can, and you will!

Just as every treasure chest has its own key, each one of you has yours. All of the women mentioned in this book have been blessed to have identified their life's purpose. Everyone has her own story, and that makes each of us unique. Life, like a treasure hunt, has a beginning, middle, and end. Of course, there is an entire journey within each phase.

How Conditioning Affects Our Identity

Ivan Pavlov was a Russian physiologist best known in the psychology field for his principles of classical conditioning. He won the Nobel Prize for Physiology or Medicine in 1904. In a now-classic experiment, he rang a bell at the same time he fed a dog. After repeating this process several times, the dog began to salivate at the sound of the bell, connecting these two events.

When we first arrive in this world as innocent and loving newborns, we look out with awe. Our conditioning begins the moment we're born and continues our whole lives. We start to gain insight from our external environment—from family, friends, school, social media—showing us what to do and how to act. Like in Pavlov's conditioning experiment, we're rewarded if we act a certain way and start to change our behaviors. These societal pressures can lead us far away from who we really are. Our identity becomes incongruent with our internal nature. We begin to mold ourselves into who we think we should be and who we're told to be, not who we want to be and who we're supposed to be—especially if we're meant to be the hero of our own story.

For centuries, humans have been awestruck by superhero stories. From myths and legends to the real-life stories of people rising above adversity, we all crave the story of a hero who overcomes great obstacles and comes out the other side a winner. Everyone has a book they can't put down, a movie or TV show they can't stop watching, or even a favorite celebrity or influencer.

You are subconsciously attached to all of these characters, and they become your heroes. While you may not sense that you have an internal hero within, you do. I would argue that the more challenges you've encountered in life, the bigger your purpose is. For example, as I shared in my earlier story of having had my arm severed, it was how I chose to interpret this event and others that ultimately shaped my destiny. At the time, I was not aware that these life events were merely clues for what my life purpose would ultimately become.

These events sharpened my ability to become a clue catcher, and eventually a clue connector. Once I was able to recognize the clues, examine their deeper meaning, and connect the dots, the road map toward my life purpose became clear. I was able to use my knowledge to unlock my own treasures. This will happen for you as you begin to implement the exercises within this book and further sharpen your own abilities.

Modern-day events have proven that not all heroes are fictional. Do you ever wonder why kids are so happy? They believe that their favorite heroes are real. Their clouded judgment allows them to create a reality where they are truly themselves. Or perhaps it is our judgment that is clouded. Contrary to popular opinion, everyone has the potential to be a hero. You could be the next hero, and you could save the world.

The concept of the Hero's Journey was first postulated by Joseph Campbell, an American writer and professor studying comparative mythology and religion. He found a universal pattern in hero tales from every culture. In the beginning of most stories, authors introduce the hero and then throw something at them that is a great source of conflict, which takes the hero into a whole heap of trouble and challenges. After facing many foes and overcoming various obstacles, the hero saves the day and comes out stronger than they were before.

The Hero's Journey concept is based in both mythology and psychological development and the actualization of one's own potential. The Hero's Journey requires a transformation of the old self and creation of the new self. The journey encompasses honor, love, freedom, approval, and survival. You'll have to overcome limitations and setbacks as you battle both inner and outer demons, confront the darkest parts of yourself, and find the treasure within you. Once you've completed the journey, you'll be ready to take on the world. This journey will not be easy—no treasure hunt is.

The 12 stages of the Hero's Journey, presented in the following chapter, will provide you with your golden compass or vision of the bigger picture. As you learn to navigate through these stages, there will be steps that you can take to ensure that you successfully propel yourself to the next stage. These steps are outlined in part II. They act in concert with one another, and all are equally important.

As you begin to master the steps, coincidently, you will start recognizing clues along the journey. The steps outlined in this book will become your treasure hunting equipment. The clues that you begin to recognize will become the dots on the map that lead you toward the treasure. In addition, once you find the treasure, you will need to locate the key to unlock the ultimate prize. The key will be discussed later in the book. You can't successfully complete the treasure hunt without all of the aforementioned tools.

We can't control all the things that happen to us, but we can control our reactions to them. Are you ready to begin the most exciting hunt of your life? Let's get started and move further into Step one of the journey.

Melissa Butterworth
CEO, ENTREPRENEUR

MY SECOND CLUE: FLASHBACK

1986 Richmond, Virginia

One summer when I was in high school, I was driving around with a group of friends trying to find some of the others kids we went to school with. We weren't old enough to drink, and we usually hung out at the local mall, skating rink, or parking lot of the local Burger King.

On this particular evening, we decided to go by one of the local sports bars and hang out in the parking lot outside. I needed to use the restroom but wasn't old enough to get into the bar to use their establishment. The closest bathroom was at least five miles away, and I was in one of those situations where I couldn't wait. I did what I believe that most people would have in this awkward situation. I jumped out of the car and proceeded to hide behind a bush while my friend stayed on the lookout to ensure that no one else could see me.

While I was behind the bush, a police officer shined a giant bright light on the bush and proceeded to approach me. I was terrified and my heart felt like it jumped out of my body. I don't remember much from that evening, other than feeling completely humiliated. Instead of letting me go, he decided to arrest me and press charges for what he called "indecent exposure." He told my mom that if I had been a man, he could have understood the situation. My parents had to hire an attorney, and I had to stand before a judge and explain myself. The level of humiliation rose to an entirely new level as I stood shaking before a judge trying to explain what happened that evening.

The judge dismissed my case, realizing that I was hardly guilty of an offense that justified a record. However, he did make me serve 160 hours of community service that summer. I was relieved but angry that the judge allowed the police officer to get away with his feminist comments. I took responsibility and served all 160 hours of work that summer.

I was bummed at the time, because I had to work the entire summer while my friends spent their free time playing tennis, hanging out at the beach, and doing all of the normal teenage activities. However, I ended up working that summer for a local blood bank, and the lessons that I learned that summer turned into opportunities and clues for uncovering my life's purpose.

I learned that I was a natural at helping others and loved the feeling I got from connecting with people and comforting them. This was the beginning of my career in the medical field and, more specifically, in the blood business.

So when you fail or hit a roadblock, don't be upset. Instead, celebrate. It only means you are one step closer to uncovering the clues and finding the key to your own hidden treasure.

CLUE

"If you run into a wall, don't turn around and give up. Figure out how to climb it."

—MICHAEL JORDAN

2

THE 12 STAGES OF THE HERO'S JOURNEY

Step 1(continued): Understanding Where You Are

This chapter takes a broader look at the various stages you'll encounter throughout life, helping you determine which stage you're currently living in and where you should strive to be. As with any treasure hunt, the ultimate goal is to find the special key that will unlock your treasure.

The 12 stages can represent any number of areas in your life—relationships, career, life purpose, spiritual development, health, finances, or any other area you may be currently focused on.

It's important to recognize that you may have already gone through these 12 stages at some point in your life in one area, only to find yourself right back to stage 1 during a different time in your life. Not everyone will go through all 12 stages, and they won't always be encountered in order either. Everyone's journey is different. For example, don't be surprised if you find yourself going through stages 1 to 5 and boomeranging back into stage 2.

The important point is to immerse yourself in understanding the 12 stages. This level of awareness will assist you in identifying where you are at any given moment and where you need to improve. While this book will focus on helping you find your life purpose, you can apply these stages to other areas in life once you understand them.

Once you have an understanding of the 12 stages of the Hero's Journey, in the next chapter, we (my featured profile authors and I) will discuss steps for you to work on mastering as you move through the different stages in your life. As we work on mastering these steps, we will take you through various exercises to uncover your strengths, talents, and ultimate purpose. Of course, as we are navigating through this exciting journey, keep alert and take note of the clues along the way. Each stage of the journey is a very important piece of the bigger picture and vital to finding the key that will unlock the hidden treasure in your life.

Stage 1: The Ordinary World

This stage is best characterized as the beginning and the "still sleeping" stage. You find yourself drifting along the currents of life and may have a sense of major dissatisfaction in several areas of your life. For example, you may be hanging out with a particular group of friends at school who aren't the best influences in your life. You might be skipping school, partying a little too much, or noticing that your grades aren't as good as you know they should be.

If you have already started your career, you may be going out to bars after work, partying too much or simply feeling stuck in a dead end job. If you're somewhere in the middle of life, and have always been a stay-at-home mom, you may feel as if you have lost your purpose. And if you are the woman who gave years of your life supporting others, you may now be facing the idea of reinventing yourself.

At whatever stage, you know inside that something needs to change, yet inertia keeps you stuck, and you're heavily influenced by friends, family, society, and social media. You don't see a clear path forward and feel as if life is passing you by.

In this ordinary world, you stay silent and suffer alone. You have a sense that you're destined for something much greater and know you're settling for mediocrity. This is the stage before the hero's story begins.

You may or may not experience a life event that catapults you into moving from stage 1 to stage 2. Most people need a striking life event to wake up. For example, you may be faced with repeating a year in school if your grades don't change, or perhaps you've gone through a recent breakup with a boyfriend. For me, one of the events that woke me up was having to serve community service during the summer that my friends enjoyed hanging out doing recreational activities with their friends.

I can remember feeling bored during high school and never feeling like I fit in with anyone. I made some poor choices and would start hanging out with a group of wilder girls. My life was going nowhere quickly as a result of my choices. After the situation with the police, I spent months living in the victim stage. Looking back at the situation, this was God's way of redirecting my path. It was my own personal awakening and transition to stage 2 of my own Hero's Journey.

Stage 2: The Call to Adventure

The call to adventure is the triggering point, an epiphany of sorts. This stage is where you experience a spark of curiosity about the world, your reason for being here, and how to overcome anything that you might be struggling with. You have the sense that it's time to start a new journey or make a major change. You feel a need to make a major shift in your life, but you are unsure what this entails. This could mean changing to a different school, career, work environment, or group of friends.

This new adventure means that you'll have to leave behind your familiar territory, depart from what you already know. You're going to have to take risks. It's time to travel to the world of the unknown. You have a sense of restlessness and excitement about what's to come.

For example, after I spent the summer doing community service working at the blood bank, I made the decision to change high schools. It was a difficult decision because I was leaving behind familiar friends, teachers, and my daily known routine. Even though my routine wasn't the best for me, it was still the known. The unknown was scary, and while I knew I had to do it, I was still resisting change.

Changing schools ended up being the best decision I could have made. I had to drive over thirty miles a day to my new high school, but the change was exactly what I needed, and things began to shift in a positive direction for my life. This didn't happen overnight, but when they did, life began to flow naturally as if a signal from the universe was saying that I was on the right path.

C L U E

In order to fly, you have to let go of
the world you're hanging onto.

Stage 3: Refusal of the Call

This stage is known as the resistance stage. You are ready to embark on this new adventure of self-discovery and mastery. However, your ego and familiar surroundings have a strong hold on you. You might be experiencing a battle between who you currently are and who you're meant to become. You're stuck in victimhood and want to move forward but aren't quite ready to face your own demons. You're curious but stuck in fear. You want to reach self-actualization, but something inside of you is holding you back.

For example, while I knew that my prior high school friends were not the most positive influences in my life, I slowly started to let go of many friendships, one by one. I changed high schools and began making other positive changes in my life. However, I continued hanging onto some relationships that weren't healthy for me, only because I was afraid of the unknown. I allowed fear of the unknown to keep me from realizing my full potential.

It took me a full year to fully recognize as I bounced back and forth from being a victim of my own circumstances to fully letting go and starting fresh. In retrospect, by hanging onto my past, I was only hurting myself.

Stage 4: Meeting Your Mentor

Your mentor can show up in many different forms. It could be someone you randomly meet, or someone you already know and admire. Your mentor could come in the shape of books, inspirational videos, or self-development courses. These mentors will become guides on your path of self-discovery. They have wisdom from their own experiences, and you'll rely on this for help along the way.

For example, one of my first and current mentors is a gentleman by the name of Gary Huff. In 2001, he was being promoted to the corporate office of a laboratory company that we both worked for. The company that I was working for had sold to the laboratory that he was working for, and I ended up taking over the position that he'd served in for several years. He handed me a hard drive containing all of the documents that he'd worked on during the five years that he held the position. The documents on that hard drive taught me more in the four years that I worked there than any other human being could have.

Gary is brilliant, and it was he who (indirectly) mentored me to become the top sales director in the company for four consecutive years. He was one of my clues and would end up showing up in my life at many critical moments. I am proud that Gary and I have remained friends all of these years and am convinced that God brought us back together to help lab owners maximize the value of their laboratories by aligning our paths once again.

Stage 5: Crossing the First Threshold

This is the stage where you've decided to leave the past behind and embark on a new journey of transformation and self-actualization. The difference between this and stage 2 is that you are now mentally prepared to move forward. You've made the commitment and will now take action.

The first task in this stage is to fight with your old belief system. However, unlike stage 3, when you were stuck and refused to change, you're now in action mode and have identified areas in which to change and grow. This stage contains a series of tasks and tests that you'll need to complete in order to advance your growth. One of those areas might be learning to develop more confidence in yourself. Or perhaps you need to start having a more positive mindset (you would be surprised how important that is).

Once you clearly define your life's purpose and realize that you have a choice in creating your new life, you'll slowly start detaching from your old beliefs. In this stage, you start to gain momentum and clarity to forge your path to the key that will unlock your treasure.

CLUE

"When you get what you want, that's
God's direction. When you don't get
what you want, that's God's protection."

Stage 6: Tests, Allies, and Enemies

Tests, allies, and enemies come in many forms, just like mentors. You will encounter risks, failures, and challenges in this stage. This may be a time when you are letting go of old friends, relationships, and other people who are not aligned with your path. These people will be those who do not support or understand your journey or have had a negative impact on your path. As difficult as it may be, this sometimes includes family members.

At this stage, you have confronted the most difficult challenges and are on your way to the key that will unlock the treasure. You will learn how to focus on the good and celebrate the blessings of failure and your most difficult times. This is an essential skill for finding your own treasure.

Let's hear from Sally and learn how she managed to successfully navigate through some of the tests she encountered through her own professional journey.

Sally Ragsdale
VICE PRESIDENT, UBS FINANCIAL

There were hurdles in my career that were hard, very hard! When I look back today, I realize that I suffered extreme abuse and misconduct from my all-male coworkers.

At the time (the late 1970s), I just thought it was the norm, the way it was. I knew that men weren't suffering as I was, but I just wrote it off and told myself that it is what it is. I didn't think there was a thing in the world I could do about it (and there probably wasn't).

Two incidents stand out vividly in my mind. Like what they say on TV, reader discretion is advised.

The first one happened during my first few months working as a stockbroker, as we were then called in 1979. I was talking with five or six coworkers (all men) about different sales tactics. One of them said, "Sally can get the clients. All she has to do is spread her legs apart." The worst part of it was, since that kind of conversation was so commonplace, I don't even think I was horrified.

Another type of incident happened more than a few times. We attended many out-of-town conferences and seminars. A number of us would walk into a hotel to check in, and I would be the only woman in the group. Inevitably, one of the men would tell the clerk that I was staying in *his* room.

As I sit here reflecting, I have deep compassion for the LGBTQ community, of which my son is a proud member. What they went through in the late 1970s is probably much worse than anything I had to endure.

On the plus side, I guess we have come a long way, baby. Maybe. Thank goodness!

Stage 7: Innermost Cave

This is where you begin deep internal work and the healing of old wounds. You'll find that through this work, you begin to develop real, long-lasting strength. You'll begin to challenge your old beliefs and that inner voice that makes you keep doubting yourself.

While you began challenging old beliefs in stage 5, you're now much stronger and believe that you can quickly identify and silence the inner critic. You will discover your identity and become even closer to reaching self-actualization.

Stage 8: Ordeal

During this stage you may begin to experience a final test of faith and patience. It's similar to stage 6, but it's the final test to ensure your faith is built on a solid and sustaining foundation.

You may feel as if everyone in the world is against you or that you've hit rock bottom. It's common to identify with this stage if you're feeling loneliness, sadness, depression, or confusion. This pain is simply another test to see if you're ready to progress to the next stage. Once you've passed this test, you'll move to stage 9.

Stage 9: Reward

The key to the treasure is right around the corner. You've committed to the process, and the universe will reward you. Remember, what you put into the universe is what you get out of it. These rewards will come in various forms including materialistic rewards, love from friends or family, feelings of happiness, and an internal sense of peace. You'll begin to see the fruits of your labor. What you're doing is starting to pay off.

Stage 10: The Road Back

The road back is an amazing time to reflect on your journey and how far you've come. It is time to celebrate all of your growth. You now have the tools needed to address any trying situation that life throws your way. You've made tremendous growth in many areas, and once you do this, you can accomplish anything you set your mind to. Everyone has gold inside of them; you just have to find it and treasure it.

Stage 11: Resurrection

The journey is coming to an end. You are a new person and are rising to self-actualization. The wisdom you've gained is embedded in your mind and heart. You're enlightened, awake, and fully connected to your inner being.

Stage 12: Return with the Elixir

When you've reached this final stage, it's time to bring all of your knowledge forward to help other people with their own personal journeys. You can share your challenges, battles, and wounds, and how you've overcome them. You can become an inspiration for others.

***

You can go through the Hero's Journey once in a lifetime or over and over again in different areas of your life. Sometimes it even happens in the same area of your life at different times. For example, I was fortunate to find my life purpose during my thirties after being fired and going through the 12 stages of the Hero's Journey. I have spent fifteen years growing a successful medical mergers and acquisitions (M&A) firm and have inspired and helped hundreds of business owners.

Over the last two years, I have uncovered a new life purpose of helping this next generation of women uncover and live their life's purpose. I didn't have to go through all 12 stages of the Hero's Journey the second time around, but I did experience some aspects of the various stages. The main reason one might not have to experience all of the stages is individual life experiences or having more knowledge than before.

Another reason might be your ability to recognize both the internal and external clues that the universe brings to light during the journey. Once you have tapped into recognizing clues and properly acting on them, your journey will catapult to an entirely new level. You will start to become your own clue catcher and ultimately a clue connector.

Before discovering what stage you're currently residing in, let's hear from Dr. Andrea Culliford about how she managed to successfully navigate through these various stages while uncovering her life purpose.

Andrea Culliford, MD, FACG
HCA CORPORATION

I grew up the only child of divorced parents. My mother immigrated to the United States from Germany at age twenty-one in 1967 after graduating from nursing school. She was adamant that I place value in education and hard work. She would let me escape all household chores as long as I succeeded in school. Thankfully, growing up in Fort Lauderdale, Florida, in the 1970s and 1980s, I found school easy.

When I graduated at the top of my class, most of my former classmates congratulated me on getting in to Penn State, when, in fact, I was heading to the University of Pennsylvania—the only student in my high school class accepted to an Ivy League college. There I majored in socializing, with my studies coming in second. In retrospect, I wish I had gone to a sleepaway camp to have had at least one experience of being away from home for an extended period of time. That would have provided me with a preview of the college semesters in Philadelphia as an undergraduate.

I did internships at an investment bank (for finance) and at a gallery (for art consultancy), and I'm glad I did, because they helped me decide what I didn't want to do. These types of detours (as I refer to them) are important because life is not a straight path. I am grateful for these experiences as much as the time I spent watching operations and volunteering at a hospital—the path I eventually pursued.

After graduating with a degree in European history, I stayed at college in the post baccalaureate premedical program to buckle down and take the all-consuming premedical courses required for medical school. I was ready to apply myself to become a doctor as I had wanted to do during high school.

I hadn't been ready to engulf myself in studies as an undergraduate because it would have required immense dedication, and I wanted to have fun for four years. Every semester that I enrolled in biology and chemistry 101, I immediately headed for the door, realizing that I wasn't going to give those weed-out classes the complete attention that they required. I knew I would fail, so I postponed my goals. I don't regret these decisions to this day and highly recommend a post baccalaureate premedical path in favor of having life experiences.

Medical school is two years of a grind of classes with lots of memorization and two years of more practical hands-on experience in a clinical setting. It helps to decide what field you want to go into as soon as possible. After matriculating at the University of Miami, four years flew by. Before I knew it, my next step was an internship and residency at New York Hospital, Columbia University Medical Center. The good thing about medical school and choosing a profession as a doctor is that it's a very well-defined path, for the most part.

After three years of internal medicine, I spent a year as a hospitalist admitting patients to the inpatient ward of New York Hospital's Columbia University Medical Center campus. It wasn't fulfilling for me personally, so I knew I was headed for specialization. I chose gastroenterology because it wasn't only using your brain to solve clinical problems but also doing procedures using your hands and eyes. Again, three more years flew by with long days that began at 6:00 a.m. and nights on call that could end at 1:00 a.m.

I recommend letting your superiors know that you have a goal of moving up in the chain of command if you have aspirations of doing so. Be assertive if you want more. It crystallizes your goals and gives you confidence by stating exactly what it is that you are striving for. It may lead to disappointment, but it also leads to getting what you want out of your career.

After a few years at my first job out of fellowship, I decided to be assertive and asked hospital leadership if I could lead the gastrointestinal (GI) division as its chief. I became the head of the gastroenterology department by year four out of training and led the division to double its number of procedures.

Good communication and being fair were my two guiding principles. I took equal amounts of on-call shifts for my group and maintained that I was there to be a shoulder to lean on as opposed to a commander giving orders. I think my colleagues appreciated this, especially coming from a woman, when the rest of my division were men. Additionally, maintaining morale is key, as jobs in medicine are so demanding. Many leaders don't understand this. Respecting people's time off and keeping meetings at or shorter than the allotted time are integral to succeeding in today's workforce.

Professional and personal growth are important to everyone. The pandemic pushed millions of Americans (myself included) to reevaluate what is important and shape their future path. During COVID-19, I realized it was time for me to grow, so I decided to leave New York City and move back to my hometown of Fort Lauderdale, Florida. A new chapter and new beginnings are awaiting me as I'm starting a job in a newly formed GI division at a new hospital in Plantation, Florida. I'm excited to bring my knowledge and experience to a new place and have that environment encourage new growth for me professionally and personally.

Medicine is one of the most challenging yet rewarding fields a student can enter. But before you decide whether becoming a doctor is right for you, it's important to research all the steps necessary to become a physician. This career is definitely not for everyone. It requires huge investments of time, money, and effort. If you still think that this is the right path for you, be sure to spend some time shadowing or being mentored by a physician for a summer. This will help to further solidify your decision before you invest large amounts of time and resources.

It's time to uncover what stage you are currently living in so we can help you navigate onward and upward.

EXERCISE

Identifying Which Stage You're Currently In

This exercise will help you to gain a better understanding of where you currently reside within each area of your life. It will assist you in identifying the areas that you need to focus on as you move forward toward the next stage. Think of it as the big picture or the ultimate treasure hunt.

Once you have uncovered the stage that you're currently residing in, the following chapters will discuss important areas to master as you progress through successive stages. In addition to mastering each of these areas, be sure to take note of certain clues that arise through your journey. These clues may be through various people you encounter, places you visit, events that occur, hunches, or your intuition.

In order to determine where you are within the 12 stages of the Hero's Journey, let's examine a few areas. Write the answers down in your journal so you can check in with yourself and your progress.

1. On a scale from 1 to 10 (with 10 being the highest), how satisfied are you with your current life?

2. After reviewing the 12 stages of the Hero's Journey, what stage do you think you're currently in? What actions could you take to propel yourself to the next stage?

3. Rate how satisfied you are in each category on a scale from 1 to 10.
   - Health, including fitness and eating
   - Hobbies and outside activities
   - Time management
   - Career or school
   - Spirituality and personal growth
   - Life purpose/understanding what you're meant to pursue in life
   - Personal relationships with friends, family, and significant other

4. What could make life better in each category?

5. What are some actions or beliefs you could implement today to improve in each of these categories?

Follow the Clues

- Treat this book as if you're starting your own treasure hunt. By completing the exercises within, you will uncover your life purpose. Your mindset will be the most powerful tool along this journey, so make sure that you maintain a positive attitude and remain true to your core values throughout the process.
- The first step toward finding your life purpose is to understand the 12 stages of the Hero's Journey and to identify where you currently reside. These stages can apply to all areas of your life.
- The concept of the 12 stages of the Hero's Journey was created by Joseph Campbell, a writer and professor of comparative mythology and religion. The 12 stages are these:

1. Ordinary World

2. Call to Adventure

3. Refusal of the Call

4. Meeting Your Mentor

5. Crossing the First Threshold

6. Tests, Allies, and Enemies

7. Innermost Cave

8. Ordeal

9. Reward

10. The Road Back

11. Resurrection

12. Return with the Elixir

- Life events can change the trajectory of our lives; keep a positive and open mind and trust that everything is happening for your own good. Learn through the hard times and use the experiences as knowledge and power. Instead of becoming a victim of your circumstances, view these challenges as clues leading you toward your destiny.

- Pay attention to the people and the clues that come into your life, as they can be your gateway to your treasure.

- We can't control all of the things that happen to us, but we can control our reactions.

PART II

3

YOUR GUIDING COMPASS

Step 2: Recognize the Power of Your Subconscious Mind

Boundless riches surround you if you're willing to open your eyes and recognize the treasure within yourself. There is gold within each of us that we can use to access everything we need to live an extraordinary life.

There are two types of people: those who know they were born to win and succeed, and those who are full of anxiety, fear, and doubt.

What is the secret to your destiny and future success? How can you be sure to be the woman who knows she was born to win and succeed? The answer is simple, yet we humans have made it unnecessarily complex.

The secret is found in your own subconscious mind. You possess the power to tap into your life purpose and to create more confidence, wealth, joy, happiness, and whatever you want. Your mission is to first become aware of this hidden treasure and then learn how to connect and release the powers within the subconscious mind. After all, you wouldn't dare start a treasure hunt without a compass, would you? A compass has a magnetic needle that indicates direction. Think of your subconscious mind as the magnet that sets the course for your life's journey.

The most amazing part is that you need not acquire anything, as you already have your hidden treasure within you. The key is to understand the process and learn how to tap into your internal resources. By doing the exercises in this book, you'll find your hidden treasure.

Your reactions to your life experiences, events, circumstances, and actions are the result of your subconscious mind. It's really that simple. If you are constantly thinking of harmony, peace, wealth, health, and happiness, wonders will happen in your life. On the contrary, if you are constantly thinking about being sick, unhappy, and less than others, your life will be filled with such things.

The key to changing your life is changing your thinking. The key to changing your thinking is to become aware of what you're spending your time thinking about.

CLUE

"Everything is within your power,
and your power is within you."

—JANICE TRACHTMAN

The Mind Is Your Secret Garden; Make Sure to Plant Seeds of Prosperity

You have one mind with two distinct parts: the conscious mind and the subconscious mind. Both play a significant role in whether you are currently living your best life, as Natalie Bohin explains in her blog post, "The Science Behind Affirmations; The Power of Autosuggestion." Think of your mind as a farm. You are a farmer and are planting seeds (thoughts) in your subconscious mind all day long—whatever you're thinking throughout the day. As you sow in your subconscious mind all day, so shall you reap in your life.

Every single thought that you have is a cause, and every event becomes an effect. Once you become consciously aware of this, it is essential that you learn how to take charge of the seeds you are planting. Therefore, to grow a beautiful garden, your mind must think constructive, powerful, positive, and harmonious thoughts.

Understanding the interaction between your conscious and subconscious minds will enable you to transform your entire life. More simply put, if you wish to change external circumstances, you must change the cause: what you're saying to yourself throughout the day. To successfully remove negativity, anxiety, and confusion, you must remove the cause: how you're currently using your conscious mind. The way that the two work together is fascinating. The subconscious mind is subject to what the conscious mind is telling it. That is why it is considered subjective.

This is why step 2 of your journey toward discovering your life purpose is to recognize the power of the subconscious mind. I was eighteen when I learned the significance of this. My mother gave me a book called *Think and Grow Rich* by Napoleon Hill. I read the book twenty times, and I started applying the principles immediately.

Once you understand the power of the subconscious, it's important to become aware of what seeds you've been planting in your mind. This level of awareness (and then what you do with it, step 3) will become the foundation from which you will rise to conquer every aspect of your life, including these areas:

- Gaining more self-confidence
- Overcoming anxiety and depression
- Tapping into your life purpose
- Mastering the ability to think positively and attract anything that your heart desires
- Attracting and creating an abundance of wealth
- Meeting the perfect partner or spouse
- Getting into the college of your dreams
- Acing any exam
- Attracting the perfect mentor, coach, or friends into your life
- Landing the career of your dreams
- Creating a healthy body image and a healthy lifestyle
- Being able to successfully relinquish control of the outcome to the universe

Be Aware or BEWARE

Let's take our understanding of the subconscious mind a step further. Once the subconscious mind accepts an idea, it begins to execute it. This fact should be a major wake-up call. Why? This rule can work for good and bad ideas alike. This is why becoming aware of what our conscious mind is telling our subconscious is so critical. When you fill your conscious mind with warm, positive, loving, and uplifting thoughts, your subconscious will act accordingly, and life will suddenly become amazing. If your mind is filled with thoughts of negativity, illness, inadequacy, anxiety, depression, and defeat, so shall life become.

The bottom line is that peace of mind, self-confidence, and a healthy body are inevitable when you start shifting your daily thoughts to reflect such ideas.

We gather our thoughts from a variety of areas—our experiences, family, TV, news, books, and friends that are closest to us. It has been said that we are the amalgamation of the five closest friends we have surrounded ourselves with. Think about your five closest friends. Do you like the implications of that statement? If not, think about making some changes to the friends you associate with.

Melissa Butterworth
CEO, ENTREPRENEUR

MY THIRD CLUE: FLASHBACK

1989, Jacksonville, Florida

I didn't have the best experience in high school and couldn't wait to attend college, as far away from my hometown as possible. Perhaps it was the crowd I hung out with in school combined with the fact that my parents got divorced when I was a senior. I only had one or two real friends and always felt different than everyone.

I was 5 feet 11 by eighth grade, didn't wear makeup like the other girls, and always felt awkward. Most of the boys didn't give me the time of day, and many thought I was a teacher and not a student. I knew deep down that I was destined for success, so moving away from my hometown was something I had to do. It was my intuition (a clue) that guided me to Florida. I initially considered moving to California, but Florida had been an area that my family traveled to as a young kid when my brother and I played in tennis tournaments. There was something about Florida that felt comfortable to me, and I was naturally drawn to the ocean.

I became aware of the power of the subconscious mind when I first starting experiencing severe anxiety in college. It started with anxiety attacks when I took timed exams, and eventually escalated into full-blown panic attacks when driving the car over any bridge. I got to the point where I wasn't able to fly on airplanes and eventually could not leave the house. I would have massive anxiety just thinking about facing any of those events.

I knew that I had to make some changes to overcome these obstacles and started searching for answers. The answers to my issues came back to the thoughts that I was allowing to enter my subconscious mind. The thoughts were ones of worry and fear, and all negative in nature. I had replayed the event of my severed arm, parents' divorce, and feeling of being a misfit in high school over and over in my own mind. I was also living a thousand miles away from home and was lonely. I had continuous thoughts of victimhood consuming my life.

I didn't feel like I had anywhere to turn, and at the time didn't know God like I do today. There were plenty of clues placed in front of me through people that appeared in my life, but I choose to ignore them.

For example, I had an Aunt Betty who took great interest in my life at the time. She would visit me during these challenging days and asked me to go to church with her and to start reading the Bible. I also had a neighbor in college who attempted to do the same things (another clue). I was too consumed in being a victim and allowed my anxiety to get the best of me. I had to hit rock bottom before I started to take any action. Looking back, I was stuck in stage 3 of the Hero's Journey, Refusal of the Call. I knew I could do better, but was allowing fear and victimhood to overwhelm my life.

As a solution, I eventually immersed myself into reading. I read dozens of books, including *The Power of Positive Thinking* by Norman Vincent Peale and *Think and Grow Rich*, as I mentioned earlier by Napoleon Hill. I started immediately applying some of the tools you're about to learn. The characters in these books became my mentors and allowed me to eventually move into Stage 4 of the Hero's Journey.

Of course, my life situation didn't change overnight, but I was eventually able to function with minimal anxiety and successfully learned how to catch myself when I was allowing negative thoughts to enter into my subconscious. I not only learned how to stop thinking the negative thoughts but eventually learned how to successfully change them with positive thoughts.

I am thankful for having experienced the anxiety and depression at such a young age. It was something that was put in my path to teach me how to successfully overcome obstacles while allowing me to learn new techniques to further enhance my own life—hence teaching it to millions of others who might experience some of their own challenges. Learning how to control the thoughts that we allow into our subconscious is at the core of every successful person. Learn to be thankful for your challenges and embrace what lies on the other side of them. It's a choice.

Are You Planting Seeds of Prosperity?

One of the most critical factors to living an amazing life is to become conscious of what you're saying to yourself. For example, have you ever dropped something and caught yourself saying, "You're so clumsy?" Or perhaps you said something when you shouldn't have and reacted harshly toward yourself by thinking, "You're so dumb." I recommend Don Miguel Ruiz's *The Four Agreements* for more about mindset and self-talk.

In addition, we must become conscious of what other people say to us. It's not so much their comments but rather what we accept as the truth that matters. For example, if someone says something about you that you know to be inaccurate, you need to reject it as false, not allowing it to enter your subconscious.

It may be harder if someone chooses to say something hurtful about us and we happen to be insecure about that specific aspect they're bringing to light. However, it's important to start being aware of when this is occurring and to recognize that we have a choice as to whether we allow this to affect us. This can be easier said than done, depending on whom we have surrounded ourselves with. We need to become aware of the people we let into our inner circle and what we are exposing ourselves to on a daily basis.

For example, are we surrounding ourselves with people who support and encourage our ideas, or people who try to pull us down? Are we exposing ourselves to media that are negatively affecting our mood? Or have we surrounded ourselves with inspirational books and media that speak words of motivation and encouragement?

From the time we were little, our subconscious may have picked up negative suggestions from those close to us. At the time, we were likely not aware of the difference between the conscious and subconscious mind and what we accepted as truth. Have you ever heard anything along these lines?

- You can't do that.
- Nobody cares what you think.
- It's no use to even try.
- You're not the smart one in the family.
- You're too old/young to do that.
- Never trust anyone.
- Watch out, you might fall.
- You're going to fail.
- Don't eat that, you'll get fat.
- Girls don't do that.

Once we have allowed these types of thoughts to enter our subconscious, we must become aware and learn how to use constructive autosuggestion to change these thoughts on a conscious level. Autosuggestion is a technique that, when applied, will release us from the negative verbal conditioning that might otherwise take us down a negative path. There are numerous techniques used in autosuggestion, but the most effective one is through affirmations (both techniques are discussed in detail in the next chapter).

We must first identify what seeds we have been planting to know what needs to be dug up and replanted. It's time to toss out the old seeds and plant seeds of prosperity.

CLUE

"Positive thinkers create large
pictures of what they want in
their minds and can predict the
future from the present...Dream
big. See your bigger picture."

—ISRAELMORE AYIVOR

EXERCISE
What Have You Been Telling Your Subconscious Mind?

Take some time to reflect on where you are in your life and then answer the following questions in your journal.

1. What types of movies, TV shows, and social media have you allowed into your life? Are these media creating good or bad thoughts? Are there some things you need to change? If so, what?

2. What are some of the hurtful messages you received as a child that you still believe about yourself today? Review the previous list of hurtful comments and see if any of these negative suggestions spark a memory or feeling within you. For example, when I was fifteen years old, the kids at school made fun of me for being too tall. They called me Big Bird. It made me feel sad at the time. Take some time to think about your own situation. Once you've identified how these things made you feel, ask yourself if you still feel this way and reflect on how you would prefer to feel. For example, today, I am very proud of being tall and feel blessed that God gave me this amazing gift. It took me several years of working on my prior childhood feelings around being tall. I first had to become aware of my feelings associated with this and slowly began to change my thoughts through the power of affirmations.

3. What have you been telling yourself recently?

4. Were you aware that you were telling yourself these things?

5. Is your current life reflective of what you've been telling yourself?

6. Are there some messages that you need to change about what you've been telling yourself? Be specific and list these.

7. Is there a common pattern or theme you're telling yourself?

8. What have others been telling you about yourself that you've allowed or accepted as true?

9. What areas of your life could use some improvement? Make a list of all the thoughts that immediately come to mind. Once you have your list, narrow it down to the top three areas that you wish to make changes in. Your list may include the following:

- How you're currently speaking to yourself
- How you've allowed others to negatively affect you
- The time you're spending on social media or watching negative TV shows
- A combination of the above

CLUE

"Perseverance is the hard work
you do after you get tired of doing
the hard work you already did."

—NEWT GINGRICH

Before we move to the next chapter and step 3 of the process: learning how to reprogram the subconscious mind toward purpose and prosperity, let's hear how Heather programmed her subconscious for success, while recognizing the clues along her own journey.

Heather Signorelli, DO

VP AND CLO, HCA HEALTHCARE

My name is Heather Signorelli. I was born and raised in Mobile, Alabama, and moved to California as a teenager. On some level, I've known I wanted to be a doctor since I was in fifth grade.

I had two amazing role models at home. My stepdad (who raised me and whom I call Dad), was an OB-GYN with a solo practice who delivered babies day in and day out. During high school he would let me come on deliveries with him and experience what it was like to work hard and bring life into this world.

My mom was a nurse who climbed her way up the corporate ladder and ended her career as vice president for a national surgery center group, running operations for a large multisite surgical hospital system.

My parents taught me that nothing worth having was easy. They also taught me, by example, that I could accomplish anything that I put my mind to. I never wanted to take the easy route in life. In middle and high school, I was determined to skip two grades and start college at sixteen. After college I spent a year or so working and learning about clinical research and, shortly after, started applying to medical schools. During medical school rotations I could envision what I wanted my career to look like. I knew I wanted to make a difference on a big scale but wasn't quite sure yet how to get there.

I went to medical school at Touro University California near San Francisco, where I became a doctor of osteopathy (DO), and then completed a pathology residency at the University of Colorado.

My residency training was geared toward physicians who were going to practice traditional anatomic pathology. For most, this involves reading slides, helping diagnose complicated cases, and being part of the care team. While this work is extremely noble and intellectually challenging, I wasn't sure that was where I wanted to be. I loved clinical pathology—running and operating high-quality laboratories was my passion.

I completed a fellowship in clinical pathology at the University of Utah. I spent my residency and fellowship years focused on laboratory management, quality laboratory operations, and appropriate test utilization. I am board certified in anatomic, clinical, and chemical pathology. My passion is in the clinical laboratory, helping to create a more efficient and effective atmosphere to practice laboratory medicine and serve our patients and healthcare system.

I started out in private practice in Denver, Colorado, as a clinical pathologist. This isn't a typical role for a private practice group because the income generated without reading slides was limited. Over a period of about six months, I worked to get contracts with three of the large healthcare systems in the area to be their system medical director. My role involved building clinical utilization committees and helping to operationalize consolidation and standardization within the laboratories nearby.

During that time, I was fortunate to know an individual at one of those three healthcare systems, Hospital Corporation of America (HCA), who believed in me more than anyone. This individual would end up being one of my clues that I was on the right path toward living out my life purpose.

Within a year or so in private practice, I was hired by HCA. I am grateful that others saw value in the work we were doing, and today I am the first vice president and chief laboratory officer for HCA. I have clinical oversight of over 185 hospital laboratories and am working with the president of lab services to develop the first laboratory service line in the company's history.

In 2015, I was a recipient of the American Society for Clinical Pathology's 40 Under Forty Pathologists award. In 2018, I received a Choosing Wisely Champion award for our nationwide laboratory utilization work.

I am grateful for the opportunity to work with an amazing team at a company that can impact change at such a large scale. I live with my supportive husband and kids in Denver, Colorado. Balancing life and work is never easy, but the opportunity to change the landscape of the lab in a large community healthcare system is more than I could have dreamed of.

With the ability to identify a goal and stick with it, no matter the challenge or barriers in front of you, you truly can accomplish anything.

Follow the Clues

- Step 2 toward discovering your life purpose is to recognize the power of the subconscious mind and to become aware of what you've allowed to enter your subconscious. Once you have this level of awareness, you can proceed to step 3 of your journey.

- You have one mind with two distinct parts: the conscious and the subconscious mind. Your mind is a farm, and you're planting seeds (thoughts) in your subconscious mind all day long.

- Once the subconscious mind accepts an idea, it begins to execute it. This is why it's important to feed your mind positive thoughts through your conscious thinking.

- The mind is your secret garden. Make sure to plant seeds of prosperity.

- Take some time to complete the exercise in this chapter to learn what you've been telling your subconscious mind and what needs to change.

- *Autosuggestion* is the term used to describe the suggestions we give ourselves. *Heterosuggestion* is the term used to describe suggestions we receive from other people directly or indirectly.

- Autosuggestion is simply a technique that, when applied, will release us from the negative verbal conditioning that might otherwise take us down a negative path. The most effective technique is through the power of affirmations.

- The secret to your destiny and future success is held within your subconscious mind. The key is to understand the process and learn how to tap into your internal resources.

- All of your life experiences are the reaction of your subconscious mind to your thoughts. Your thoughts create your reality.

- The key to changing your thinking is to become aware of what you are thinking about.

- Having basic knowledge of the interaction between your conscious and subconscious mind will enable you to transform your life.

You are starting to see the treasure off in the distance and understand the bigger picture. You are knowledgeable about the 12 stages of the Hero's Journey and understand where you currently reside and wish to be. You understand the difference between the conscious and subconscious and have become aware of the significance of what you're telling yourself repeatedly throughout the day. You are aware of the people, places, events, and things that you've been allowing to enter your daily life and the impact they have in your life.

4

BOUNDLESS TREASURES AWAIT

Step 3: Using the Law of Attraction to Train Your Subconscious Mind

It's time to embark on step 3 of the process, which includes implementing various techniques that will help program your mind for success. If you started a treasure hunt, your mind would be full of excitement and anticipation as you imagined all of the boundless treasures that were there for you to claim. The key is to learn how to have this same approach to life on a consistent basis.

Take a moment to congratulate yourself for making it this far. It's important to take moments to celebrate where you are in the journey and how far you've come. This will allow you to become more grateful and inspire you to keep going. This next step is the most exciting and magical one yet.

CLUE

To paraphrase Henry Ford,
whether you think you can or
cannot, you are correct.

Melissa Butterworth

CEO, ENTREPRENEUR

MY FOURTH CLUE: FLASHBACK

2007, Miami, Florida

I am a self-made multimillionaire, twice over. I don't say that to impress you, but to impress upon you that if I can do it, so can you. It took me fourteen years to achieve the first time and seven the second. I know exactly how I became a millionaire and subsequently lost it within a year. It is the realization that I am about to share that allowed me to become a millionaire the second time—in half the amount of time—and maintain that label.

I had not fully comprehended step 1 or step 2 of the process outlined in this book—my place in the 12 stages of the Hero's Journey and what I was allowing to enter my subconscious mind on a daily basis. Therefore, I lacked the essential foundation to sustain wealth long term. For example, when you have no understanding of the bigger picture or the stage of life you're currently living in, it's hard to know where you're headed.

I had achieved success at a young age but was stuck in stage 6 of my own Hero's Journey. I had been fired from my dream job and was facing many tests in all areas of my life. I made bad decisions about the people I was surrounding myself with and didn't recognize the clues that the universe was sending my way. Instead, I wallowed in my own self-pity, allowing myself to become a victim of my own story.

After being fired, I stayed in stage 6 for several years. The story that I allowed into my subconscious was a negative one, and it continued to play over and over again, like a broken record. I had allowed myself to go down a negative spiral that would eventually propel me into a black hole of endless despair. I kept telling myself that I wasn't good enough. I chose to direct my anger about what had happened to me by spending millions to prove my employer had deceived me.

Looking back, I was stuck in stage 6 of the Hero's Journey, Tests, Allies, and Enemies. In addition to being stuck, I had not learned how to fully manage my own finances. For me, this was the equivalent of starting a treasure hunt without a compass or map and being lucky enough to stumble upon the treasure. When I found the treasure, I didn't know what to do with it. I had jumped right to step 3, learning how to use the mind to attract wealth, and had made millions.

It was the summer of 2007. I was thirty-four, single, and a multimillionaire making seven figures, living in my ocean-front luxury home. Prior to that, I'd spent years working eighteen-hour days, living in a small one-bedroom apartment, and driving a beat-up Saturn. There were times when I didn't know how I was going to pay my bills. I had come a long way and worked hard to make my dreams a reality.

Suddenly, everything in my life came to a screeching halt. I was fired from a dream job for supposedly having a "side real estate company" that was considered a corporate conflict of interest. At least, that was the company's side of the story. Their side of the story changed several dozen times through-out litigation.

As with any story, there are two sides. My side was that I had gotten permission to have a real estate website, and in my mind, there was nothing competitive in nature between real estate and medical blood sales. Even though I had been the number-one sales producer in the entire company for five consecutive years, they used this excuse to fire me.

I was faced with several choices in the weeks following being fired: I could go work for the competitor and bring my loyal clients to that company (I did not have a noncompete agreement), find another job somewhere else, or start my own company. After speaking with four attorneys, I was told that I had a legitimate case against my employer. I made the decision to start my own company and sue the company that had fired me.

The decision to start my own company was the best decision I could have made. Suing my prior employer was the worst decision I made. I struggled with both decisions.

It took over three years to get my business off the ground, and only one year to spend millions of my hard-earned money supporting my lifestyle while growing my business and supporting what seemed like an army of attorneys.

The decision to sue caused me to lose all of my financial wealth. However, I still had my knowledge, proven track record, and industry contacts. It would take me seven years to regain what I'd built over fourteen years and subsequently lost over the course of twelve months. The lawsuit would continue for nine more years. For those considering entering into any lawsuit, don't do it. The legal system in this country is a disaster, and the only ones who win are the attorneys. On the flip side, starting my own business was a blessing. However, at the time, it was a struggle.

When you hear "rock bottom," you think of losing everything. Unfortunately, I had officially hit it, dead on. When you hit rock bottom, it's not fun. You feel as if there's no way to climb out, no matter how hard you scratch and claw at the situations around you. However, if you're ambitious and determined to make failing a learning experience, rock bottom will allow you to grow into a stronger person than you were before. I read, learned, and applied the principles outlined in this chapter until they became second nature.

While going through this experience, I was thankful for the decisions I had made years earlier in my life. For example, while my friends were out partying in college, I spent countless days and nights reading, attending motivational seminars, taking outside courses, journaling, and applying all of the steps you're about to learn. That's right: if you master step 3, you can and will become a self-made millionaire.

However, let my story be a warning for you. It's crucial that you build a solid and sustaining foundation and follow each and every step in this book. If you are trying to find the treasure and skip a step, you may never get there. And if you skip a step but happen to stumble upon the treasure, you'll be susceptible to losing it all.

> **TREASURE HUNTING RULE**
> *Ignoring a clue may prove*
> *to be disastrous.*

The Law of Attraction

The Law of Attraction is a philosophy that suggests positive thoughts bring positive results into a person's life, while negative thoughts bring negative outcomes. The Law of Attraction teaches that thoughts are a form of energy. It's that simple.

The Law of Attraction is the most powerful law in the universe and must be understood before anything else can be of value. Everything that you are achieving or not involves the Law of Attraction. If you wish to live life to your fullest potential, this law must be brought to a clear level of consciousness. Rhonda Byrne's *The Secret* is a good source for more about the Law of Attraction.

As we discussed, it is imperative to become aware and to comprehend how your thoughts, actions, and feelings contribute to your destiny. Once this level of awareness is achieved, you'll start to recognize that those people who speak about illness are attracting more sickness into their lives. Those who speak about prosperity and success will attract success and prosperity. It's that simple.

Before we dive further into this principle, let's hear how Dr. Heather Signorelli applied this principle to her own unique career path even though others told her that it would be impossible.

TREASURE HUNT RULE

Pay attention when you have a big dream in your heart and soul.

Heather Signorelli, DO
VP AND CLO, HCA HEALTHCARE

When someone says you can't do something or that it's impossible, do you believe them, or do you forge on?

In residency, soon after I had my first child, I remember sitting down with the attending physician and sharing what I envisioned my career looking like as I planned for fellowships. I was told what I wanted wouldn't be possible and that I needed to stick with traditional training and change the plans for my fellowship.

While I know their intentions were good, I was told that being a clinical pathologist in private practice wasn't something anyone would pay for. However, I intuitively knew that I wanted to be on the business side in a community healthcare system. I wanted to be in operations, dealing with process improvements on a large scale. My intuition was one of my clues.

So I found mentors who had chosen alternative career paths and learned from their experiences. I sought out opportunities to serve on committees such as those with the College of American Pathology. In addition, I started a consulting business during my residency. I found a community filled with individuals who were doing what I was told was impossible. I worked hard and learned from anyone who would teach me.

I was grateful to find a few others both in residency and early in my career who believed in what I wanted for myself. They were clues helping me along my path toward my own treasures.

I continued to read and learn how private hospitals could benefit from improved efficiencies in the lab and about trends in reimbursement. I created a niche for myself that truly helped me get my first job out of fellowship.

Seeing the need for a more business-focused approach in medicine, I began to plan for ways I could help clinical laboratories become more efficient and more profitable. I knew that healthcare waste was an increasing problem, and waste in-laboratory was no different. Looking back, it was this relentless attitude and commitment to not giving up that enabled me to get where I am today. I am now the first vice president and chief laboratory officer for the largest healthcare system in the country.

I truly believe that if you have the mindset that you can do anything, even the impossible, you will accomplish great things. Unrelenting hard work and planning lead to success. My dad always said, "Be careful what you wish for." I not only wished for this career, I believed in it, I planned for it, and I executed it.

CLUE

"You become what you believe."

—OPRAH WINFREY

Once you understand that you will become what you believe, the next step is to apply several proven techniques that will help to program your mind for success. The first technique is positive affirmations. We will start with this technique in order to reprogram some of the things you've allowed to enter your subconscious mind. You should already have a list of the top three areas that need improvement in your life, so let's get started.

Positive Affirmation Technique in Five Steps

According to the National Science Foundation, the average person has 12,000 to 60,000 thoughts per day. Of those, 80 percent are negative and 95 percent are repetitive thoughts. Positive affirmations are one of the best techniques to reprogram negative thoughts. It's as simple as replacing negative statements that you've been feeding to your subconscious throughout the day with positive statements. Think of it as replacing poor eating habits with healthy choices. Make sure to focus on one of the three areas that you wish to change at a time.

Here are the five key steps.

STEP 1: IDENTIFY YOUR NEGATIVE STATEMENTS

Take the top three areas you're looking to make changes in, from the prior exercise, and write out the negative statements you were previously telling yourself. For example, you may have been saying, "I am so fat" or "I will never be that thin."

STEP 2: CREATE YOUR POSITIVE AUTOSUGGESTIONS

Once you've written out the negative statements you've been saying to yourself, it's time to replace them with something positive. Rewrite each negative statement as a positive autosuggestion, using the following guidelines:

- **Your autosuggestions must be in the present tense.** For example, if you're looking to become physically fit, you wouldn't say, "I will become healthy and fit this year." You would say, "I am healthy, active, and physically fit." The key is to keep things in the present moment.

- **Your autosuggestions must be positive.** The subconscious only responds to positive commands—"I am a confident person" as opposed to "I am never nervous." If you wish to become healthier, you might suggest, "I am in great shape and perfectly healthy," as opposed to "I really need to lose some weight." The key is to practice reframing things positively.

- **Your autosuggestion must be believable.** To successfully reprogram your subconscious mind, you must believe that you can. Initially, this may feel uncomfortable, and you'll have to continue practicing. It might even feel like the cliché "fake it until you make it." As we've learned, most people spend their day thinking negative thoughts. If you wish to change and live a harmonious life, you must believe that you can and will, starting today.

- **Attach emotions to your autosuggestions.** The subconscious mind is greatly influenced by our emotions, so it's helpful to imagine how you'll feel once you achieve your end goal. Make sure that you put sincere emotions behind what you're saying. The more emotions you attach to your autosuggestions, the better the results will be, according to author and speaker Napoleon Hill.

STEP 3: RELAX YOURSELF THROUGH MEDITATION

Meditation is the formal process of setting time aside to train the mind through connecting with your breath. There are countless ways to accomplish this, but your breath awareness should be the focus.

Find a comfortable, ordinary chair, sit in an upright position, relax your shoulders, and settle your body. Close your eyes and bring your full attention to your breath. Begin by taking three full, conscious breaths.

Focus your attention on inhaling deeply and holding that breath for a moment before exhaling through your mouth. Try not to think about the past and stay present. You can count down from 50 to 1, or visualize the vibrant colors of the rainbow. Be sure that you remain in the present and focus on your breathing. The key is to get yourself into a comfortable meditative state where you connect with your subconscious.

Once you are in a comfortable position, move on to step 4.

> **TREASURE HUNT RULE**
> *The key to meditation is getting connected to your soul. Be sure to listen to your inner voice. It will relay important clues for your journey.*

STEP 4: REPEAT YOUR POSITIVE AUTOSUGGESTIONS, WITH FEELINGS

To reprogram prior negative thoughts, focus on one of your newly created mantras (your autosuggestion statement can be a mantra) and say it out loud. Repeat to yourself, for example, "I am healthy, active, and physically fit." You might repeat this out loud numerous times. Be sure to add emotion as you focus on the end goal.

For example, think about a time when you were in the best physical shape of your life. Close your eyes and recall a time when you felt strong, happy, and proud of yourself. You might consider smiling and pat yourself on the shoulder as you relish in the moment. Perhaps this moment was captured in a photo and you can remember how amazing you felt at that exact moment.

The key is to connect with the feeling. It's important to stay in that emotional state and make that feeling a dominant one for as long as possible.

STEP 5: PRACTICE, PRACTICE, PRACTICE

The best way to reprogram the subconscious mind is through daily repetition. The key to becoming a success in any area is through daily practice. You must practice until you've successfully reprogrammed your thoughts.

EXERCISE
Autosuggestion

1. In your journal, write out three goals you want to accomplish in the next year.

2. For each goal, write positive autosuggestions using the steps previously outlined.

3. Meditate and repeat your autosuggestions three to four times a week for the next month until they become so ingrained that you are automatically planting seeds of greatness.

Creative Visualization Techniques

Creative visualization is the process of imagining exactly what you want in your life, as if you've already achieved it. You are in essence creating an inner experience of what it would be like to have your desires become a reality. This is slightly different from the positive affirmation technique because you're putting emphasis on the visualization rather than on the words themselves.

There are many ways to practice visualization. This section includes some effective exercises that I have used over the years.

BASIC VISUALIZATION

1. Pick a time of day when your mind is most rested and you feel like you can focus.

2. Pick a goal, something that you desire to do or have. For example, "I would like to be more athletic."

3. Make an affirmation about yourself as if it has already occurred. It is helpful to use the present tense and keep it simple. For example, "I am an athletic person."

4. Close your eyes and picture your goal while allowing yourself to feel as if it were already true. Make sure that you connect with your emotions. As you are visualizing, feel the emotions as if what you are visualizing has already happened and you are remembering what it felt like. The key is to allow yourself to feel what it would be like to be athletic. Picture yourself running on the beach, lifting weights, or whatever feels right for you.

5. In the beginning, do this for ten to fifteen minutes a day, three to four days a week. As this exercise becomes more natural, increase the frequency until you're doing this naturally every day.

TREASURE MAP TECHNIQUE

A treasure map, similar to a vision board, is a physical picture of your desired reality. It's one of my favorite visualization techniques and likely the most effective I've encountered. It's valuable because it forms a clear image of your ultimate goals. I compare it to building a home and having an architect put together a blueprint for the project. Just like a blueprint, you'll have a sharp image of your life's goals.

There are many ways to create your treasure map, including these:

- Painting on a canvas
- Cutting out positive words and inspirational pictures from magazines and cards and creating a master collage
- Creating a digital board on your computer with words, pictures, and other visuals that inspire you

The goal of the treasure map is to create a snapshot of your ideal life so that you see this vision of yourself every day. Some basic guidelines can help assist in the creation of your treasure map.

1. Make your treasure map whatever size works best for you. I typically make a 10 x 12 poster board on January 1 every year. It's become my New Year's Day tradition. I know some people who keep it in a special notebook or create it on a standard 8.5 x 11 sheet of paper and fold it to fit in their wallet. Everyone will have something different that works best for them.

2. Try to limit your treasure map to one or two specific goals, allowing your mind to focus on what's necessary to achieve them. Building multiple maps for separate goals may work better, or you can create an all-inclusive universal map. I recommend creating a treasure map for each of the following areas of your life:

   - Personal relationships

   - Financial desires

   - Career

   - Life purpose

   - Spiritual growth

   - Health and fitness

3. It is important to put a picture of yourself on the treasure map. You can draw yourself in the picture or add one of your favorite selfies. For example, if you envision being an author of a bestselling book, put a picture of yourself on a book cover and place it in the center of your treasure map. If you envision yourself traveling around the world, place a picture of yourself on an airplane and a picture of the globe in the center of your treasure map.

4. Use pictures, colors, words, and symbols that motivate you. It is helpful to include your affirmations from the previous exercise on the treasure map.

5. Once you have completed your treasure map, display it in a place that you can see every day. You might want to hang it in your bedroom, office, or any place that brings you positive energy. It's important that you take the time each day to review it, visualize your goals, and embrace the feelings that come with it.

THE HELIUM BALLOON TECHNIQUE

Have you ever purchased a helium balloon from the grocery or party store? The helium balloon technique builds on the basic visualization technique that we discussed earlier in a very simple, effective way.

1. Sit down somewhere comfortable, whether it's on the beach, indoors on your favorite comfortable chair, or outdoors in nature with your feet stable and comfortable on the ground.

2. Close your eyes and breathe deeply, becoming aware of each breath, as you count backward from 50 to 1.

3. Imagine something that you wish to manifest in your life. Imagine that this has already happened. Picture this clearly in your mind and allow yourself to feel the sensations of having already accomplished your goal.

4. In your mind, picture a helium balloon filled with all of the things that you want to accomplish: your biggest dreams, something you want to bring into your life, or an opportunity you've been hoping for. Use color to brighten your visualization: maybe a bright green balloon if you're envisioning prosperity or a pink balloon if you wish to bring love into your life.

5. Imagine the balloon is filled with all of your (future) accomplishments and then let the balloon go, floating off into the universe, while still focusing on your vision. (You may consider releasing an actual balloon into the air.)

6. You can do this practice once, daily, or once a week as a ritual. The more often you do this technique, the more your desires will come to pass.

This exercise symbolizes letting go of control over the vision and turning it over to the universe (or a higher power), allowing it to bring your manifestations to you. You are not letting go of your vision itself, just letting go of the outcome.

Remember, once you let the balloon go, it is out of your hands. The universe is now in control.

In addition to the Law of Attraction and these visualization techniques, the power of gratitude is critical for sustained success. We'll explore gratitude further in the next chapter.

Prior to exploring gratitude, let's learn how Jennifer has applied many of the techniques mentioned throughout this chapter to exceed all of her dreams.

Jennifer Tattanelli
FASHION DESIGNER AND ENTREPRENEUR

Born in Florence, Italy, and raised in a bilingual home speaking both English and Italian, Jennifer Tattanelli has devoted her entire life to crafting and designing fashion, representing the voice of a new generation of young, talented Florentine leather stylists.

Jennifer's father launched a career in fashion, starting one of the first leather goods manufacturing businesses in Italy. Jennifer's parents were very supportive of her love of fashion and encouraged her to model with the local Italian modeling organizations, including Pitti and Pitti Bimbo.

As a child model, fashion always surrounded her. In addition, Jennifer acquired a taste for American folk art from spending summers with her grandmother June Ewing, a well-known artist and folk art collector. Jennifer carried memories of June's amazing house, which was completely decorated with tavern signs, an enormous merry-go-round rabbit, an Amish carriage, dolls, stoneware, a barber shop pole, furniture, and portraits. These childhood visits were like Alice in Wonderland for Jennifer. They helped to inspire her creative and artistic side. Looking back, they were clues to her life's purpose.

Jennifer first launched her career at Calvin Klein in New York City, then returned to expand the family business in Florence. She's been working at her family's company for over twenty-five years, constantly researching new ideas and trends. She is proud of her work and her roots.

She says, "I'm extremely particular and respect the Florentine craftsmanship that is unique worldwide. I insist on handmade items being carefully cut, designed, and executed by our Florentine artisans, on the painstaking detailed stitching, on the choice of high-quality materials, and a precise assembly and final fit for the garments. I love creating new looks using refined, elevated, quality materials for my clients. This includes shoes, jackets, handbags, dresses, belts, shirts, pants, scarves, and many other beautiful items."

Living in Florence, with its treasures of art, buildings, crafts-manship, and colors, made it easy for Jennifer to develop her taste for the beauty and uniqueness of that city. Interestingly, Jennifer visualizes minimalism in each work of art, visible in her creations. She creates fashion that exudes simple elegance and expresses pride in being Italian American. The cultural influences are evident in her designs and personal style.

Jennifer and her family split their time between Florence, New York, and Palm Beach, and spend the summers in the Hamptons. Her children's smiles are her greatest inspiration. Her dreams are to keep designing and crafting. She's on Instagram @JenniferTattanelli.

Follow the Clues

- Step 3 of our journey is about understanding the power of the thoughts we feed into our subconscious mind. Four techniques that we can use to assist in our journey are positive affirmations, creative visualization, treasure mapping, and the helium balloon technique.

- The Law of Attraction is a philosophy suggesting that positive thoughts bring positive results into a person's life, while negative thoughts attract negative outcomes. It's based on the belief that thoughts are a form of energy and that positive energy attracts success in all areas of your life including health, career, finances, and relationships.

- The Law of Attraction is the most powerful law in the universe and must be understood before anything else can be of value. Everything that you are or are not achieving has to do with the Law of Attraction.

- Once you become aware of the Law of Attraction, you must work on applying it to your life. The five steps of applying the power of affirmations are these:

  1. Identify your negative statements.
  2. Replace negative statements with positive ones.
  3. Practice meditation to reach deep into your subconscious mind.
  4. Repeat affirmations with feeling.
  5. Practice, practice, practice.

- You will become what you believe.

You see the treasure off in the distance and understand the bigger picture. You are knowledgeable about the 12 stages of the Hero's Journey, can see exactly what stage you have been living in, and are elated to be progressing to the next stages. You understand the difference between the conscious and subconscious and have become aware of the significance of what you're telling yourself repeatedly throughout the day. You are aware of how the people, places, events, and things in your daily life impact your thoughts and enter your subconscious mind.

Through the prior exercises, you have identified areas you need to improve upon and have begun implementing techniques to attract greatness into your life. You're starting to recognize that some of the things that you have been focusing on have started showing up in your life. You're more excited than you have been in a long time. You know that you are on the right path.

5

CELEBRATING EVERY STEP OF THE HUNT

Step 4: Applying Gratitude to Your Daily Life

Do you believe in magic? Remember when you were younger and full of excitement when you lost a tooth because the tooth fairy would be coming that night? You couldn't wait to wake up the next morning and check under your pillow to see how generous she had been. You counted down the days until Christmas or Hanukkah or your favorite holiday, waiting for a bit of that magic to enter your life.

The toys that we played with had names and sometimes matching personalities. If we had pets, they were like people to us. Our imagination had no limits and life was magical.

As we grew into adults, the responsibilities of life—bills, rent, family, school, SAT scores, marriage, jobs, bosses, and maybe even kids—started to take their toll on us. We began to doubt that the magic we once believed in as children still exists. So many people say they wish to be young again, when everything was magic and ponies, but just because you've grown up doesn't mean there isn't magic everywhere around you.

What if I told you that the magic that we once believed in as a child was real, and that the disillusionment of adults is what is false? I'm not saying that the tooth fairy exists, or that reindeer fly, but I am saying that you can and will experience all your dreams when you start to implement the practice of gratitude. You may not ever fully know how everything weaves together to make your dreams come true, but that is the beauty of magic. It works in the invisible realm and is tied to energy within the universe.

Are you ready to experience magic in your life again? I think it's safe to assume that most of us would embrace this. Let's get started with step 4 of our journey, implementing gratitude into our lives. Let's first hear from Cheryl and how she learned the importance of gratitude in her own life.

CLUE

When we apply gratitude on a regular basis, we will be given more. If we fail to practice gratitude, the many things that we have to be thankful for may start to vanish.

Cheryl Adelman

ENTREPRENEUR, ORGANIZE IN A DAY

A PAINFUL LESSON ON THE IMMEASURABLE VALUE OF ACCEPTANCE, APPRECIATION, AND GRATITUDE

Some years ago, I was taking hot yoga three to four times a week at 6:00 a.m. It was difficult and challenging. Just completing the class was an achievement.

I was stretching, improving, and incorporating the lessons of yoga into other areas of my life. I was learning the valuable lesson of getting comfortable with being uncomfortable, a great lesson for business and life.

Taking hot yoga became part of my identity. It was good for me—mind, body, and soul.

Another important lesson they taught is that if we are staying in form, challenging ourselves consciously, then we are getting 100 percent value no matter where we are in the posture. I remember to apply this concept to my business today.

Perfection is an unattainable goal, the beacon. Experiencing the process is where the value lies, so staying in form and challenging oneself is the actual goal. As a metaphor, this is true for us as entrepreneurs.

Time went by. I injured both my shoulders (unrelated to yoga). And I stopped doing yoga. But during the first weeks of being home during COVID-19 confusion, I tried a few online yoga classes to help myself deal with the uncertainty around income. Friends in different cities were in touch recommending their favorite online teachers and classes.

It has great value sharing ideas with an extended circle. In business we are not alone and it is essential to have people we can share ideas with.

I see now that going to class was enough. I am enough! I had been "in the arena," as Brené Brown says in *Daring Greatly*, based on the quote by Theodore Roosevelt. "Showing up" had all the value in the world.

I had to experience the pain to understand that. It was a hard lesson.

I accept where I am. I appreciate where I am. I strive to stay in form. This thinking is good for business. My mentor tells me to keep going. She is one of my clues in my journey.

For me, this experience is a powerful lesson in being present, in accepting and appreciating what is. The road was never meant to be easy. It was meant to be worth it.

CLUE

"It is not the critic who counts: not the man who points out how the strong man stumbles or where the doer of deeds could have done better. The credit belongs to the man who is actually in the arena, whose face is marred by dust and sweat and blood, who strives valiantly, who errs and comes up short again and again, because there is no effort without error or shortcoming, but who knows the great enthusiasms, the great devotions, who spends himself in a worthy cause; who, at the best, knows, in the end, the triumph of high achievement, and who, at the worst, if he fails, at least he fails while daring greatly, so that his place shall never be with those cold and timid souls who knew neither victory nor defeat."

—THEODORE ROOSEVELT

Sir Isaac Newton, one of the greatest scientists of all time, made many scientific discoveries in the 1700s, including the fundamental laws of motion in the universe, one of which helps us better understand the importance of gratitude: every action has an equal and opposite reaction.

When you apply gratitude to Newton's law, it says that every action of giving thanks causes an opposite reaction of receiving. Have you ever noticed that when someone laughs around you, you start to smile and laugh too? The same applies when you bring positive and ambitious people into your life. We tend to take on energy similar to that of the people we surround ourselves with.

How Magical Is Your Life?

Are you currently living a magical life? Your answer will indicate exactly how much gratitude you've been applying to your life. For each area on the following list, write down a number from 1 to 10 that represents how magical your life is (10 being the most magical).

- Health
- Happiness
- Finances
- Home
- Relationships
- Career
- Life purpose

For example, maybe you've recently experienced what you'd call a streak of good luck. You aced your finals at school, landed your perfect summer job, and feel like everything is going your way. Perhaps you've recently started working out more, have lost a lot of weight, and feel the strongest and healthiest you have in years.

The areas that you've rated as highly magical are those that you've most likely applied gratitude (and action) to. For example, you've been working out and eating healthy (action) while saying a gratitude mantra of, "I'm so grateful for the health and strength of my body, mind, and spirit." Any areas that are not abundant and wonderful may be that way due to a lack of gratitude. It's really that simple.

The combination of action and gratitude allows you to achieve your goals and live a magical life beyond your wildest dreams. That's right—you're your own magician and are in control of creating or stopping the flow of magic in your life. In order to receive, you must give. It's the law. Gratitude is giving thanks, and without it, you cut yourself off from receiving everything you want in life. Remember, when we don't have gratitude, what we currently have will be taken.

Recall my earlier story about having personally lost millions over the course of one year. That was the result of some poor decisions combined with the fact that I had taken my own financial success for granted. I had not spent time and energy giving thanks for those blessings. As a result, it was quickly taken from me.

The universe responds to whatever thought, emotion, or action you put out. If you wake up in the morning and stub your toe as you're getting out of bed, then yell or become annoyed, you're sending this energetic vibration to the universe and the universe will respond accordingly—as you go about your morning routine, you run out of toothpaste, you don't have time to make a healthy breakfast, you feel rushed, and your hair isn't doing what you want it to do. Then you start driving and traffic seems to build for no reason. Well, the reason is that you've sent out the vibration of frustration and annoyance to the universe; the universe is giving you more of those experiences because it doesn't know the difference between what you want and don't want. It only knows vibration.

Now, let's say you get out of bed and stub your toe one morning, and instead of getting worked up over it, you brush it off, laugh, and say, "Today is going to be a great day!" You continue your morning routine and although little inconveniences may occur, you're not tangled up in them because you've sent a clear signal to the universe that you're going to have a great day. The universe responds accordingly.

Maybe you get to school or work early that day and have time to get a healthy breakfast before going in. Or you show up to work or school and your best friend has brought you a cup of coffee and breakfast by surprise. Your hair stays in place all day, you have fulfilling interactions and meaningful conversations throughout your day, and so on. The possibilities are endless! What you put out, you receive. And this doesn't have to start with your morning routine.

It's normal to go back and forth from feelings of gratitude to anger, annoyance, and an entire array of feelings. But anytime throughout the day, you can change your thoughts, feelings, and emotions. The best way to put this into practice is to send out a positive thought of gratitude and let negative emotions go. Trust that the universe has received your message loud and clear and be open to receiving validation of your thoughts throughout the day.

A simple mantra may be, "I am open to receiving the gifts of joy and happiness that the universe, angels, and guides have for me today. May my eyes be open and my heart full." You may even want to place your mantras on simple index cards and carry them in your bag to look at throughout the day or on your smartphone. Another benefit of being a positive person (and one filled with gratitude) is that you'll go about life that much happier.

CLUE

"No duty is more urgent than
that of returning thanks."

—JAMES ALLEN

EXERCISE
30-Day Gratitude Challenge

If you want to make a change in your life, start by taking the following 30-day gratitude challenge. This is where step 4 of your journey begins.

Start on a Monday morning when you first wake up and give thanks for as many things as you can. Do it again right before going to bed that evening. Repeat this daily for thirty days until it becomes a habit.

You may find yourself giving thanks for some of the same things on a day-to-day basis, adding new items on other days. The key is to start giving thanks for what you have and where you reside in your life at this exact moment.

When you start implementing this exercise, think back to the things you're looking to create in your life. For example, if your life purpose is to start a business in fashion, then your daily gratitude should focus on actions that are already leading you closer to recognizing your fashion dreams. Not quite sure where to start?

BUILDING A GRATITUDE HABIT

Try these three ways to practice gratitude. I suggest that you start with the gratitude journal for the first week and then slowly add in the other two steps—one during the second week and the other during week three.

- **Write in a gratitude journal every morning and night.** The moment you wake up, list the first ten reasons you're thankful. For example, write out, "I am blessed to wake up this morning and to have my health." Always end your sentence with, "Thank you!" As you write out the top ten reasons you're thankful, say them out loud. The key is to allow yourself to feel thankful. Complete this same exercise before you go to bed at night and reflect on the events that occurred during the day that you are thankful for. Complete this exercise for thirty days in a row, until it becomes a daily habit.

- **Do something nice for someone else one or two times a day.** This could be as simple as paying for the person's coffee behind you in the Starbucks drive-through or complimenting someone on their outfit or hairstyle. It could entail sending a card to your mom or dad to tell them how special they are. Another simple act of kindness is to take the time to listen to others throughout the day. Listening is a skill that very few people learn to perfect. There are many lonely people who could use a friendly ear. These simple acts of kindness and ways of showing gratitude will do wonders for you and the other person.

- **Take the time each day to tell one or two people how much having them in your life means to you.** Let them know how much you appreciate them and be specific. For example, if your parents have taken the time to help you with an important project, tell them how much you appreciate them and give them a hug or a special handwritten card.

Make gratitude an everyday part of your life. Allow being grateful to become a natural part of your personality. You will start to see magic happening in all areas of your life that you continue to give gratitude toward. If we get caught up in life and forget to practice gratitude, the magic will start to vanish. You'll be able to recognize which areas you haven't been practicing gratitude in—versus areas in which you have—simply by looking at your existing circumstances. If you start noticing a few problems occurring in your life, you should immediately increase gratitude in that area. The universe will give you subtle signs about the energy you're radiating. If someone in front of you at the Starbucks drive-through buys your coffee, you can sit back and smile, knowing you're putting out positive energy.

Through the practice of gratitude, you're applying one of the most important laws of the universe. It's simply a gift from the universe that's there to advance your life. We tend to think of the universe as separate from ourselves, but once we realize that we possess the power within ourselves, we can work wonders in our lives. You can become a channel for unlimited blessings.

Gratitude is the cure for broken relationships, poor health, lack of money, fear, grief, depression, and worry. Gratitude brings solutions to problems, enabling you to create opportunities and realize all of your dreams.

Follow the Clues

- Step 4 of our journey begins with implementing daily habits of gratitude. Whoever has gratitude will be given more, and they will have an abundance. When someone does not have gratitude, what they have will be taken from them.
- Experiencing magic in our life starts by implementing daily gratitude.
- We tend to take on a similar energy to those that we surround ourselves with.
- Take the 30-day gratitude challenge. Make gratitude an everyday part of your life. Make being grateful a natural part of your personality.

> **TREASURE HUNT RULE**
> *Take action on your clues.*

6

KNOWING THE TREASURE IS YOURS

Step 5: Creating a Positive Mindset

Congratulations. You can see the big picture and have a clear understanding of where you have been stuck. You know where you desire to be and are learning the tools that will assist you in getting to your desired result. This next step of your journey is another key to making sure that you have the tools necessary to embrace any and all of life's challenges.

Are you a glass half-empty or half-full sort of person? Studies have demonstrated that both can impact your physical and mental health and that being a positive thinker produces more desired outcomes.

A recent study in the *American Journal of Epidemiology*, "Optimism and Cause-Specific Mortality," followed 70,000 women from 2012 to 2020 and found that those who were optimistic had a significantly lower risk of dying from several major causes of death, including heart disease, cancer (breast, ovarian, lung, and colorectal cancers), infection, and respiratory diseases.

Other proven benefits of thinking positively include these:

- Better quality of life
- Higher energy levels
- Better psychological and physical health
- Faster recovery from injury or illness
- Fewer colds

- Lower rates of depression
- Better stress management and coping skills
- Longer life span

Positive thinking won't make all of your problems disappear. In fact, before positive thinking can occur, you have to allow yourself to process the negative emotions. After all, we know how difficult it is to jump to positive thoughts when we get cut off in traffic, receive some bad news, or have a tough day.

Instead, we can allow ourselves to experience the feelings of anger or frustration and then take five deep breaths with the intention of releasing those feelings with our exhales. Once we have accomplished this, we can replace the negative thoughts with positive ones such as "I'm so glad that God is protecting me today." Or "I'm so glad that I can enjoy such a beautiful day." Positive thinking can help make problems seem more manageable and allow us to approach hardships differently.

When you harness the power of positivity, it's amazing the impact that it has in your life. It can decrease stress and increase self-confidence. It can make every moment worth experiencing. By thinking positively, you just can't help but be optimistic, even if others around you are negative.

As a result, you are less depressed, happier, and more satisfied. The benefits of positive thinking are vast.

Let's hear directly from Ellen who chose to focus on the positives in life and turned her own vision into a billion-dollar brand.

Ellen Latham, MS

FOUNDER, ORANGETHEORY® FITNESS

With more than forty years in the fitness industry, I have built a billion-dollar brand out of a lifelong passion. My no-nonsense approach whipped devoted fans into shape, both in the fitness studio and in life. In my book, *PUSH*, I shared the three keys to living one's "ALL-OUT" life, with my life's mantra being "Look at what you have, not at what you don't have!"

I draw inspiration from my father and mentor, Arthur Calandrelli, who was a physical education teacher and football coach at my local high school in Niagara Falls, New York. My story speaks to passionately overcoming life's inevitable ups and downs and starts with me being let go from my job in my early forties, when I was a single mother of a nine-year-old boy. With degrees and certifications in fitness and the pure internal drive to succeed, I started a Pilates fitness business in a spare room in my home. I continued to build momentum until I borrowed some money to open a 1,100-square-foot Pilates studio in a local spa in my city.

After a few years working around the clock and having a relentless attitude, I decided to move to a bigger space and created what I called The Ultimate Workout. My members weren't happy with their fat-burning workouts (spinning, jogging, and cardio at the gym) and asked me to create the best fat-burning hour they could and should do.

In 2008, I opened this new studio with such excitement because I knew it was based on science, on how our human cells respond to exercise, and that it would work. I was not wrong. The word got out about this fantastic workout that produced great results, and I was very busy and very excited.

I was approached by a franchise company in 2010 to rebrand my workout with the hope of opening many of these studios. In those early days we were getting excited about opening maybe forty studios. Eleven years later, we have 1,400. Orangetheory® Fitness (our rebranded name) is now in over twenty-four countries (with eight different languages) and has had over one million members.

In 2017, Orangetheory® Fitness was number one on the Women Presidents Organization's list of the 50 Fastest Growing Women-Owned/Led Businesses in the United States. I was also honored to be named on the 2018 Forbes 50 Over 50 list, which recognizes fifty very successful women who are stepping into their power at 50-plus years of age.

I have been asked more than once what it takes to remain relevant in the same industry for over forty years. The first thing that came to mind was that you must *stay awake*. What I mean by this is that I have always paid close attention to what my industry leaders were saying and doing. I was part of every fitness-related organization that offered me insight into something I didn't know.

But most importantly, I paid attention to my members and what they were saying and feeling. I'm always trying to solve a problem that they may feel they have regarding fitness.

The second thing I did over the years was offer more value than my members expected. Whether it was my time or education, I always brought them along for the ride.

I often encourage female entrepreneurs to find their "superpower." We all have them, but women sometimes need to be reminded. So here are some pieces of advice I've given women I've coached.

Throughout my years as a female leader, I have shared my challenges with many other women, like being placed on an uneven playing field, facing gender stereotypes, having to advocate on my own behalf, needing to trust my own voice, and having to build alliances.

I've always loved the science of things. Did you know women start out with a bit of a disadvantage biologically? We have less testosterone and dopamine. These are the "reward" hormones in the human body that drive the desire to achieve and compete.

I've always coached my female executives to have great posture when presenting themselves. Use a strong voice with confidence and paced breathing when speaking (this counters the adrenaline).

Another thing that has guided me through the years is to establish a strategic track record of success. Nobody will notice when you do an easy job, but if you want to get noticed, solve a problem that no one else has solved.

Have the courage to stick with your convictions.

Know how to rebound from inevitable disappointments and always support the success of other women!

I've heard that if you want greatness, you will experience great challenges. To thrive in hard times, you need to maintain deep roots in something that will keep you strong. My vision of what and who I really want to be has always done that for me.

I also pay attention to my energy. Energy is like a radio station with a lot of channels and a lot of messages. What channel you stay on depends on what you pay attention to.

Never undermine HOPE. Hope is the expectation that tomorrow will be better than today. It is about getting up again and again.

I will leave you with the law of cause and effect. You may be familiar with Newton's third law of motion, that "for every action there is an equal and opposite reaction." Your thoughts,

actions, and reactions will determine whether you receive positive or negative effects. My suggestion? *Choose positive.* I did.

Let's jump into some exercises that will help you to train your brain to think
positively. You can use the following exercises to help you get started.

EXERCISE
11 Exercises to Help You Accomplish Your Goals

1. **Boost your mood by memorizing positive information.**

   Did you know that you may be able to boost your mood by memorizing
   lists of positive words? When you force your brain to use positive words
   frequently, you make these words (and their basic meanings) more accessible and easily activated in your brain. So when you go to retrieve a word
   or idea from your memory, positive ones will come to the top more easily.

   Not sure which words are positive? In 1999, psychologists Margaret Bradley
   and Peter Lang painstakingly measured thousands of words to determine
   how positive and negative they are. We have compiled these into a positive word chart, located on our website at www.TheAmericanInterns.com.
   If you're struggling to think positively, try this strategy first. It can help
   develop your brain in ways that make the other positive thinking strategies
   easier to implement. Some examples of positive words include these:

   · Abundance

   · Accomplished

   · Alive

   · Dazzling

   · Confident

- Courageous

- Happy

- Handsome

- Miracles

- Motivated

- Ambitious

- Excellent

- Powerful

- Exuberant

Take the next five to ten minutes to journal as many positive words as you can. Take the time to reflect on the words and their meanings and allow yourself to be in the moment.

2. **Strengthen your brain's ability to seek out positive information.**

Once your brain has built strong neural networks for positive words, try to extend these networks by asking your brain to use positive information in new ways. For example, you could set an alarm for one minute and focus on giving yourself five to ten compliments.

Or you could print out positive words on cards (one word on each card), cut each card in half, shuffle them all together, and find each card's match. For example, the word "laughter" would be cut into "laugh" and "ter." To match the word pieces, your brain has to search through lots of positive information to find what it's looking for. This positive memory recall task is beneficial for brain functioning as well as positive thinking.

3. **Direct your brain to pay attention to the positive.**

    Are you one of those people who notices the bad stuff, like when someone cuts you off in traffic or your food doesn't taste quite as good as you wanted it to? If you are, you've likely trained your brain to focus on the negative, and your brain has gotten really good at it. It can become challenging to undo this training. It's time to train your brain to become better at focusing on the positive.

    For example, if your social media feed is full of pictures of things and people that leave you feeling negative or less than, purposely search for positive images that make you feel good. For example, you could start searching for cute puppies, funny kid videos, or even positive messages. The social media feed algorithm will then start to show you what you ask it to. Sound familiar? Our social media feed can be a great example of how the universe responds to your thoughts. Make it a conscious habit to focus on positive information and direct your attention away from the negative.

C L U E

"We may encounter many defeats,
but we must not be defeated."

—MAYA ANGELOU

4. **Condition yourself to experience moments of positivity throughout the day.**

Did you know that you can condition yourself for positivity? As we previously learned with Pavlov's conditioning experiments: Pavlov would ring a bell right before feeding a dog. Over time, the dog started getting excited by the sound of that bell, even when food wasn't present. Eating food and the sound of the bell became linked in the dog's brain. Something as meaningless as a bell was now making the dog excited.

This effect is called classical conditioning. It's the idea that when two stimuli are repeatedly paired, the response that was first elicited by the second stimulus (food) is now elicited by the first stimulus alone (the bell). This happens all the time without us even realizing it.

For example, for many of us, our favorite food is something we ate as a child with our families. Likely our positive feelings of being with family got paired in our brains with that particular food. As a result, when we eat the food, we now get the warm, fuzzy feelings that we got from spending time with family, even if our family isn't present.

Although your environment is conditioning you to react in particular ways all the time, if you know what you're doing, you can use classical conditioning to boost your positivity. You do exactly what Pavlov did: you repeatedly link everyday things (like a bell ringing) with positive thoughts and feelings. For example, maybe you program the ring tone on your phone for someone you love with your favorite song or sound. Every time this person calls you, you hear that tone and allow yourself to feel a boost of positive thoughts every time you hear it. Pretty soon, these boring things will automatically generate positivity. That's classical conditioning at work. This can help you think positively, because when you're going about your life, maybe even feeling bummed about life's challenges, you'll have positive moments that keep you energized and in a good mood.

5. **Think positively but allow yourself to grieve and express sadness.**

Of course, thinking positively has its benefits. But thinking positively isn't always the best response. Negative thoughts sometimes have benefits too.

When we are sad or grieving, thinking negative thoughts and expressing corresponding emotions help us communicate to others that we need their support and kindness. When we are treated unfairly and get angry, our thoughts can help motivate us to take action, make changes in our lives, and change the world. Casually pushing these negative emotions aside without seriously considering their origins can have negative consequences.

It is important to recognize all emotions, cope with them, and try to become more positive as you focus on the hidden blessings. Think of life as your personal treasure hunt, with the bad things serving as clues leading you to the key.

Let's take a moment and hear from Tina who was able to master the art of thinking positively while allowing herself to first grieve and express sadness while she faced the fight for her life.

Tina Randall
FOUNDER, RECALL

"THE MIND IS THE MOUNTAIN THAT YOU HAVE TO CLIMB"

I grew up in Montreal, Canada, as an only child until my brother was born when I was sixteen. The same year, I started spending my summers working as a volunteer Candy Striper (a CLUE early on) at the Royal Victoria Hospital. This was the beginning of my love affair with medicine.

My first job was working with cancer patients as a hematology technician (as I remained gravitated to the medical field of caring work). It was rewarding but I had a desire to explore other possibilities after three years. I knew that some of my gifts included fashion, design, marketing and communicating with people. These skills came naturally for me. I pursued a college degree in marketing and merchandising.

I intuitively knew (an unknown gravitating force) that my ultimate destination would be South Florida. I had family and friends there and always loved the warmth of South Florida. A few months later I met my former husband and married a year later. We started a safety supply distribution company and our family.

Having a natural talent with people, and knowing that most businesses live and or die by sales, I appointed myself as the Vice President of Sales and Marketing. My life consisted of hard work, sacrifices, long hours and doing double time as a mom. I was juggling building a company in addition to being a mom. I wore many hats including businesswoman, cook, chauffeur, social director, and guidance counselor.

Nineteen years later, my life was interrupted with a diagnosis of stage 3 breast cancer when I was forty-seven years old. Simultaneously, my husband and I separated. For the first time, in a long time, I felt off balance. I was unsure of how to continue being a Wonder Woman, VP of marketing and sales, care for four children, beat and survive cancer, and transition my children through a divorce.

Outraged, I thought to myself, "I have plans and I wanted to live." There was no way that I was ready to leave. I dug in, armed myself with knowledge and strength and reprogrammed my mind. I made the conscious decision that this was merely a detour that I was going to get through. I was determined to survive. I began the fight to save my own life.

A bilateral mastectomy, high-dose chemotherapy, radiation, and reconstructive surgery. It felt like an eternity. Between fighting for my life, mothering our children, staying strong with hope and prayer, I made it through the storm. Four years after treatment was finished, I found the strength to bring closure to a twenty-four-year marriage.

As if my life had not already felt challenging enough to conquer, the courts awarded little child support for the two underage children and alimony was held back. I was shut out of the company I had helped build and my credit cards were cancelled. Oh, and with all of my health issues my health insurance was canceled. I felt devastated. While I was striving to hold onto hope, I wondered, what now?

I kept going while the children and I adapted to a completely different lifestyle. I worked in retail, did marketing for a rehab center and introduced a line of sanitizer to the cruise industry during the norovirus outbreak on cruise ships. I used every tool in my tool box to keep us going.

Eventually, I circled back to my first love, medicine. For the past twelve years, I have successfully managed, researched, and introduced instrumental health options at a concierge gynecological practice. It took me several years to understand that the challenges I have faced in life have shaped me into the strong women that I am today.

Looking back, I understand that my purpose in life has been to raise four incredible children, survive a diagnosis of cancer, be a leader in helping other women with life threatening health issues, and wake up each day thankful for what I have. However, now, at seventy-one, I realize that I have yet another purpose to fulfill.

My love of medicine and having survived the ups and downs of breast cancer have been my clues to my ultimate life's purpose. My mission is to proactively work with physician's offices and radiology centers in assisting them with ensuring patients follow up with the need for additional screenings and procedures that are required after their initial screening. It has been reported that 4 out of every 10 women who have a mammogram need follow-up exams.

This percentage does not include woman who have been diagnosed in the past and who require more routine follow-ups. Shockingly, nearly 33 percent of women are not showing up for annual testing after treatment. I have formed a corporation, RECALL that will help solve this problem and ultimately save lives. RECALL proactively manages, follows patients' schedules, and supports the patient from the point of necessity to the need to return for further testing or procedures after their annual screening.

My mission and purpose as a survivor is to ensure that patients persevere, to reassure that there is a light ahead, provide a support system, to take charge of their own inner power, and hold onto their womanhood with grace, dignity, and courage.

6. **Savor the good moments.**

Too often we let the good moments pass without truly celebrating them. Maybe your friend gives you a small gift or a colleague makes you laugh. Do you stop to notice and appreciate these small pleasures that life has offered? If not, then you could benefit from savoring.

As Dr. Tchiki Davis explains, savoring means holding onto the good thoughts and emotions we have. You can savor by holding onto the emotions you're feeling in positive moments, or you can savor positive experiences from long ago. Savoring is a great way to develop a long-lasting stream of positive thoughts and emotions.

Think of savoring like enjoying your favorite food. You love that food so much that when you eat it, you must savor it because it's too good not to. Now, apply that thought to your life and start to savor and let the good moments resonate within you.

7. **Generate positive emotions with bursts of positivity and humor.**

The broaden-and-build theory of positive psychology suggests that experiencing positive emotions builds our psychological, intellectual, and social resources, allowing us to benefit more from our experiences and be happier. So how do we infuse our lives with small bursts of positive emotions?

One way is to watch positive or fun videos. Watching cat or puppy videos or inspirational videos can generate a quick boost of positive emotions that can help fuel an upward spiral. Studies have found that laughter lowers stress and anxiety and reduces depression. It also improves coping skills, mood, and self-esteem.

Be open to humor in all situations—especially the difficult ones—and give yourself permission to laugh. It instantly lightens the mood and makes things seem a little less difficult. Even if you're not feeling it, inducing laughter can improve your mood and lower stress.

Just be sure to mentally hang on to the positive emotions that emerge through strategies like savoring, so you take your good mood with you throughout the day. In fact, we recommend taking a walk out in nature and listening to a motivational podcast or a YouTube video (but be careful not to get sucked in for too long, or you may end up feeling guilty for not getting more done).

Another way to infuse bursts of positivity into your day is to focus on the good things no matter how small or insignificant they seem. If you look for it, you can find the proverbial silver lining in every cloud—even if it's not immediately obvious. For example, if someone cancels plans, focus on how it frees up time for you to catch up on a TV show or other activities that you enjoy.

8. **Spend time with positive people.**

   Both negativity and positivity have been shown to be contagious. Consider the people with whom you're spending time. Have you noticed how someone in a bad mood can bring down almost everyone in a room? A positive person has the opposite effect on others.

   Being around positive people has been shown to improve self-esteem and increase your chances of reaching goals. Surround yourself with people who will lift you up and help you see the bright side.

9. **Practice positive self-talk.**

   We tend to be the hardest on ourselves and are often our own worst critic. Over time, this can cause you to form a negative opinion of yourself that can be hard to shake. To negate this, you'll need to be mindful of the voice in your head and respond with positive messages, also known as positive self-talk. Research shows that even a small shift in the way you talk to yourself can influence your ability to regulate your feelings, thoughts, and behavior under stress.

Here's an example of positive self-talk: instead of thinking "I really messed that up," say to yourself, "I'll try it again a different way."

10. **Identify your areas of negativity so you can begin to shift your mindset.**

Take a good look at different areas of your life and identify the ones in which you tend to be the most negative. Not sure which areas? Ask a trusted friend or colleague. Chances are, they'll be able to offer some insight. A coworker might notice that you tend to be negative at work. Your spouse may notice that you get especially negative while driving. Tackle one area at a time.

11. **Start each day on a positive note.**

Create a ritual in which you start off each day with something uplifting and positive. Here are a few ideas.

- Tell yourself that it's going to be a great day, or express any other positive affirmation. I have found it helpful to pick three positive qualities that you have (or would like to have) and create a statement that you tell yourself throughout the day. For example, "I, Mel B, am a positive, athletic, and healthy woman." Your statement might change from time to time depending on what you would like to work on at the given moment. The key is to focus on saying this out loud several times throughout the day, allowing yourself to feel the emotions that go with your positive affirmation.

- Listen to a happy and positive song or playlist. The music that you listen to subconsciously shapes your mindset.

- Share some positivity by giving a compliment or doing something nice for someone else.

- Practice daily gratitude as previously discussed.

- Consider watching stand-up comedy clips first thing in the morning. This is a fun way to ensure you start the day off with a few laughs.

How to Think Positively When Everything Is Going Wrong

Trying to be positive when you're grieving or experiencing other serious distress can seem impossible. During these times, don't pressure yourself to find the silver lining. Instead, channel that energy into getting support from others.

Positive thinking isn't about burying every negative thought or emotion you have or avoiding difficult feelings. The lowest points in our lives are often the ones that motivate us to move on and make positive changes.

When going through a tough time, give yourself grace. Try to see yourself as if you were a good friend in need of comfort and sound advice. What would you say to that person? You'd likely acknowledge their feelings and remind them that they have every right to feel sad or angry in their situation, and then offer support with a gentle reminder that things will get better.

During these challenging times, it helps to reach out to your inner circle for additional support.

Positive thinking is a critical skill and takes energy and a concerted effort every day. You won't be able to undo years of pessimism and negative thoughts overnight, but with some practice, you can learn how to approach life with a more positive outlook. It's all about rewiring your brain and making progress one step at a time. That is key to remember as you continue your journey toward finding your own treasure.

Let's hear directly from Sally who applied a positive mindset and became a leading powerhouse in the financial world.

CLUE

"Work as if you were to live a
hundred years. Pray as if you
were to die tomorrow."

—BENJAMIN FRANKLIN

Sally Ragsdale
VICE PRESIDENT, UBS FINANCIAL

I believed everything that came out of my father's mouth, so why would I not believe him when he told me that I could do anything I set my mind to? I was number four of five girls (all born within six years) and, in my opinion, the least smart. I was always an overachiever, and I guess it never occurred to me that I could have fewer opportunities because I was female (born in 1955). That wasn't even on my radar. Along with believing I could do anything, my glass was always 7/8 full.

My name is Sally Ragsdale. I'm sixty-six years old and a vice president of UBS Financial, the largest wealth management firm in the world. I love what I do, and I've been doing it for forty-two years.

Here's my story. My husband says I act like a firstborn child. I was fortunate to attend a small all-girls middle and high school. When my mother suggested an all-girls college, I said no. However, I believe strongly that an all-girls school and an all-girls family helped me to develop confidence and security without worrying about what the boys thought. You see, I was quite chubby during those years and was teased a lot by boys.

I made good grades. I was an overachiever. In high school, taking standardized tests, the remarks from the teachers were, "How does she do so well in school? Her test scores don't show that." With the confidence I got from my dad, the 7/8-full glass, and being blessed with wonderful people skills, I thought I could conquer anything.

My dream was to go to Davidson College in North Carolina. It didn't deter me a bit that I was applying the first year they accepted girls—only twenty, to be exact. There was no reason I couldn't be one of those twenty. Well, I wasn't!

Fast forward four years, and I graduated from Emory University with a degree in business. I didn't have a clue what I wanted to be, but it seemed practical to get a degree in business. That was the beginning of being outnumbered by men in my career.

I started work with the Trust Company Bank in Atlanta (now Truist). One of my assignments was as a "loaned" executive to United Way. Companies assigned a few of their employees to work for the United Way fundraising campaign, and I was one of the loanees. I was wildly successful with the accounts I was assigned to. My dad, who I suppose was my guidance counselor, said, "If you can sell a charity, you can sell anything!"

I got married, moved back home to Jacksonville, Florida, and started "peddling stocks," as my dad called it. Most people called it a stockbroker, now known as a financial adviser.

I was hired by a small boutique firm at the age of twenty-three. That may not sound unusual now, but hiring a twenty-three-year-old woman was unheard of in the investment industry at the time. (Speaking of unheard of, before I was hired, my husband had to be interviewed by my prospective boss.) I would often be the only woman in the room for the next thirty years. I was the first stockbroker at my firm to get pregnant. I would go to firm conferences and there would be just a couple of us gals in rooms of between 50 and 100 men.

In the early years of my career, I felt that I should be doing more to help people. My parents were very charity-minded and always doing for others. My husband became a Presbyterian minister in his mid-thirties. Then I realized that just because I wasn't feeding the hungry didn't mean I wasn't helping people, sometimes in a big way: helping them make wise decisions with their investments, determining how their savings should be allotted to charities, and making sure they knew how to provide for their children.

In the 1970s, the number of women who had no knowledge of investments or weren't participating in their family finances was astounding to me. I started focusing on women and empowering them to be financially independent.

I had to blaze the trail for women who would come after me. It was *not* easy. I had to work much harder than my male counterparts and still was not treated as an equal for about the first twenty-five years. I was disrespected and ridiculed, but back then, in the late 1970s and early 1980s, there were no channels to do anything about it, nor did you think you *could* do anything about it even if there were.

It was hard at times, but giving up was never an option—never crossed my mind. I loved what I did, and I loved the thrill of it. It made me tough, and there is good and bad to that. It was hard in a traditional marriage in the '70s and '80s to be that tough, but we made it through (forty-two years and counting) and had three wonderful boys.

It is now the season of change for me, and it is time to head to retirement. I spent forty-two years at the same job—you don't see that anymore. I am being called in a different direction. My husband and I lost our thirty-three-year-old son suddenly two and a half years ago. I knew from the day he died that when I was ready, I would be helping others through the grief process. So I recently started a grief counseling group for mothers who have lost children. This is my calling for this season.

Follow the Clues

- Step 5 of your journey is to train your brain to think positive thoughts. Those who are optimistic have a significantly lower risk of dying from several major causes of death including heart disease, cancer, infection, and respiratory disease.

- Other proven benefits of thinking positively include better quality of life, higher energy levels, better psychological and physical health, faster recovery from injury or illness, fewer colds, lower rates of depression, better stress management and coping skills, and a longer life span.

- Train your brain to think positively by implementing one of eleven key tips:

   1. Boost your mood by memorizing positive information.

   2. Strengthen your brain's ability to work with positive information.

   3. Direct your brain to pay attention to the positive.

   4. Condition yourself to experience moments of positivity throughout the day.

   5. Think positively, but allow yourself to grieve and express sadness.

   6. Savor the good moments.

   7. Generate positive emotions with bursts of positivity and humor.

   8. Spend time with positive people.

   9. Practice positive self-talk.

   10. Identify your areas of negativity so you can begin to shift your mindset.

   11. Start each day on a positive note.

7

KNOWING YOU HOLD THE KEY

Step 6: Developing Sustaining Self-Confidence

Each one of us has a continuous inner dialogue going on with ourselves throughout the day. We talk more to ourselves than to anyone else. As we are now aware, most of the time we speak to ourselves subconsciously without even being aware of it. The question is, what are you saying to yourself?

Many people are walking around living a mediocre life because of the negative recording they're playing in their mind. As we've learned, the key is to become aware in order to change the way we are speaking to ourselves. Pay attention to how you talk to yourself. Once you learn how to talk to yourself in the right way, you will rise to a new level of self-confidence—and that's step 6.

What Is Self-Confidence?

Self-confidence is self-discovery—finding out who you are and what you are truly capable of accomplishing. Self-confidence involves both acceptance of one's whole self and how one acts in the world because of it. It is the perfect merging of self-esteem (the degree to which someone values themselves) and self-efficacy (someone's belief in their ability to accomplish something).

Self-confidence is a process that involves how someone thinks of themselves and others, as well as how they function despite certain challenges and uncertainties. It's about being in a world that allows you to connect to yourself, take care of yourself, and love yourself. It involves understanding your strengths and weaknesses, having self-respect and the courage to tell the truth about who you are, what you will allow, and what you believe. It's all about knowing you, believing in you, and acting on your beliefs.

In many ways, confidence means having faith. Faith is an awareness of the presence and power of God within you. A person reflects confidence through posture, speech, gestures, and looking others in the eye. We are all individual expressions of the universe or the higher power we believe in. Once you learn to adopt this attitude, you'll lose any sense of inferiority. To truly master self-confidence, you must have faith in the eternal principle of life within you that created you and the world.

These statements illustrate what self-confidence can look like:

- I know that I am worthy of love, acceptance, abundance, and everything that I desire.
- I am worthy of others' respect and friendship.
- I accept the whole me, including my strengths and weaknesses.
- I am courageous enough to stand up for what I believe in.
- I know that I am not perfect and choose to forgive myself for my mistakes.
- I am complete with a sense of inner peace.
- I love and accept myself as I am.

Why Is Self-Confidence So Important?

According to research conducted by psychologist Barbara Markway, self-confidence is linked to almost everything we want in life, including a positive sense of self, our overall happiness, and success in work, school, sports, and relationships.

Tackling the demons of self-doubt is a brave and essential pursuit. At times you may feel discouraged or scared, but that just means you're on the right path. Soon you'll learn how to take advantage of fear as we review common misconceptions about self-confidence and learn what it really is, where it comes from, and how to obtain it. You'll start to understand how confident you currently are, and you'll begin setting a baseline to measure your growth.

Confidence is a mysterious quality. We often view self-confidence as the willingness to take steps toward goals, even if you're anxious about the outcome. If you break down self-confidence, it is competence, courage, and self-compassion mixed together.

As women, we can all relate to having suffered a lack of self-confidence at some point in our lives. Perhaps it was the fact that we felt we weren't thin enough, pretty enough, smart enough, talented enough, popular enough, or worthy enough. That we simply were not good enough.

CLUE

"No one can make you feel
inferior without your consent."

—ELEANOR ROOSEVELT

I think it's safe to say that at some stage in our journey we may have felt lost, on a path to nowhere, struggling to find our own direction and inner happiness. While this is a horrible feeling, it's one of the clues to figuring out your life purpose.

Our beliefs about ourselves are often shaped by the people and messages around us. However, we must realize that our self-confidence is within our control, despite the exterior circumstances.

Many people struggle with negative self-perception for a variety of reasons. Your genes, childhood experiences, and other life circumstances all play a role. While we can't change our genetics or the experiences in our past, there is plenty we can do to alter our thoughts and expectations to gain more confidence.

As you will read with Gillian's childhood experiences, she could have easily allowed herself to slip into a victim mentality. Instead, she used her experiences to further propel her toward achieving her dreams.

Gillian Lieberman
ACTRESS AND LUXURY REALTOR

"DON'T QUIT 5 MINUTES BEFORE THE MIRACLES HAPPEN"

In the second grade, I had my first introduction to mean girls. With tears in my eyes, I ran home to my mom, begging her for answers on what I could've possibly done wrong to warrant my classmates putting me down. Thus began a long, tumultuous journey of battling judgments.

At that impressionable age, my wise mother taught me a lesson that has become integral to who I am today: rise above and live in your own truth; because that's all you have. That mantra, and the guidance and inspiration from the powerful, inspiring, independent, and confident women around me has ushered me through my darkest moments over the last twenty-two years. Little did my mom know, she was preparing me to face the meanest people of all: the audience of a reality TV show.

It hasn't been all bad. As I mentioned, my tribe has always consisted of women, like my single mom, who persisted against all odds and created happy, successful, and fulfilling lives. To this day, I am constantly inspired by my mom, who has lived the life that she desires, regardless of others' opinions. My mom wanted a baby. Here I am. My mom wanted to be the president of the PTA and a full-time Wall Street financial adviser. She made it happen. In fact, she made it look a little too easy, as she overcame obstacles I didn't recognize she was facing. Perhaps she was protecting me from the dark truth that I would learn once entering the public eye.

When I signed on for a reality TV show, I understood that my words would be taken out of context in the editing room. Hollywood's intentions to craft my story into a predetermined storyline were written in black and white into the contract.Knowing what I was signing up for, I accepted the consequences.

We had several rounds of virtual interviews and a final in-person callback in LA, during which the producers asked the most invasive questions possible. I wear my heart on my sleeve without shame, so I was selected as one of the brave (and likely insane) people who would bear the intimate details of her life on national television.

We've all heard endless stories of female celebrities who were wronged by the media. Women like Britney Spears, Kim Kardashian, and Pamela Anderson had their lives excavated and their reputations defiled for the public's enjoyment. Why? One could argue that they signed up for it, much like myself. But perhaps a better examination would be why the strongest people make the best targets. Is it because they are the ones who can handle the heat and pick themselves up again?

That was certainly my experience throughout school and college. Why society enjoys demolishing women who seem to have it all is a deep-rooted misogyny that I personally don't wish to unpack. Female public figures who step into their power, despite it all, are much more interesting to me.

I lost my autonomy on my TV show. We had no contact with the outside world and we were trapped "on set" in houses and on location. Producers had plot lines set up for us that secretly led us down the path of self destruction. The people who I was supposed to trust were actors and producers lying to us. There were good people, but anything we said or did could and was taken out of context.

Being ostracized by strangers on the internet who knew nothing about the real me seemed like it would be a piece of cake. My whole life had prepared me for this. Why should I care what they think? They are haters hiding behind a computer screen merely responding to a caricature of me.

But I am only human. I read the comments; they only slightly hurt. What hurt most was pouring my heart, soul, and time into a three month twenty-four seven filming process, only to be misconstrued by millions of viewers. Imagine pouring your heart, soul, and time into a three-month casting process and a six-week 24/7 filming process, only for it to be misconstrued by thousands of viewers. Perhaps this is my ego talking, but all I wanted was for people to know the "real" me.

Then I realized something. No one will ever know the inner workings that comprise my being. The strangers on the internet don't know the real me. Even close friends and family don't know the real me. They know perceptions of who I am based on their own experiences, insecurities, and realities.

There restarted the never-ending journey of finding the balance between who I want to be, versus the boxes that others want me to exist in. People can always find something judgmental to surmise about me, no matter what I say or do, what I have or lack, etc. Am I going to continuously change myself to meet every expectation, or allow these judgments to roll off my back?

I want a robust life. A life where I try to satisfy every third party's suppositions is empty, and frankly impossible. Most importantly, my own discernments on what is best for me would fall to the wayside. That is a scary, unstable life.

So I turn to the things that make me happy. I turn to my goals, both professional and personal. I turn to my mom, my cat and my dog, my hot yoga classes, and long walks on the lake trail. I turn to journaling and therapy and the sunrise in the morning. I turn to my interests in science, performing arts, and education. I turn to my mentors. I turn to bettering myself. I turn to my vulnerability that makes me anything but weak. I turn to small joys and spiritual moments. I turn to the pride that I allow myself to feel when looking in the mirror.

I am not sorry for any parts of me, even the imperfect ones. I embrace my defects because it reminds me that I have tremendous growth to do. I humble myself to let in guidance from the people I trust, and I always stay true to what's in my heart. At the end of the day, the only person I want to impress is the woman in the mirror. Today, I am proud of who she is.

My mission in life is to take control of my narrative and inspire others to do the same. I hope to rewrite the story of the unapologetic woman who is too powerful to be controlled. Let's cut the time in between ostracization and redemption— it's boring. The generations of women before me have had to wait for their moment to take control. I will not wait.

Meet Gillian Lieberman, a twenty-two-year-old reality TV Star on *Temptation Island* Season 4 on USA Network, the creator of her own hair care brand, and a licensed Florida Realtor® with multi-million dollar listings. Gillian attended the Professional Performing Arts School in New York City and holds a BFA in musical theater. Gillian has won national awards for her appearances in New York City professional theater performances, as well as danced with the French Academie of Ballet, the Radio City Rockettes, and the Alvin Ailey American Dance School.

The Benefits of Improving Self-Confidence

Confidence is linked to almost every element in a happy and fulfilling life. The following sections detail the many benefits of improving your self-confidence.

STRONGER RELATIONSHIPS

The higher your self-confidence, the more you begin to focus on others. You'll be able to get out of your own head and be less focused on what people think about you. You'll begin to genuinely enjoy interactions with others because you won't be worried about the impression you're making. Your relaxed state will put others at ease and will help forge deeper connections. You'll begin to develop more empathy for others, and it will become evident to those around you. When you're less preoccupied with your own self-doubt, you become the person who reaches out to help those in need. You'll learn to become a better listener and people will be naturally drawn to you.

Let's take this moment and hear from Ellen who followed her passion for helping people and became a top sales executive in the computer industry. She was able to build a successful career doing what she loved and by putting the needs of others first. As a result, the money followed, and she would grow to become one of the top computer saleswomen in the country.

Ellen Butterworth
COMPUTER SALES EXECUTIVE

"LISTENING TO CUSTOMERS WILL WORK MIRACLES."

I grew up in the remarkable small city of Lynchburg, Virginia. From an early age, I learned to listen to my family, friends, and anyone who needed a listening ear. Actually, listening was the key to my successful business career!

I graduated from James Madison University with a degree in mathematics. I met my first husband in math class. After graduation we both taught math in public schools for many years. We were blessed to have a son and daughter who are still to this day my best friends. Over the years, we had two amazing grandchildren.

We moved from Harrisonburg, Virginia, to Richmond, Virginia. I was fortunate to be asked to teach math at St. Catherine's School, a private all-girls school. This is where my next adventure unfolded. I spent a lot of time helping my students, even after class. I believe in giving everything you do 150 percent. As a result, a parent of one of my math students recognized my extra initiatives and asked me if I could help him start up a new computer store. It's important to recognize the people who are placed in our path in life, as they can become catalysts (clues) to changing your destiny. I left teaching and started on a path that would help me become financially independent and able to retire in my early fifties.

It turned out that selling computers was my hidden specialty, even though decades ago I had *no* idea how computers would change the future of the world. I would go into Fortune 500 companies and listen to many technical people tell me how desperate they were to find hundreds of computers. The technical people would tell me exactly what they needed, and I would listen and place the orders. It was as simple as that. They had challenges, and I was able to come up with solutions for them.

One day, I happened to see an advertisement (clue) in an Atlanta newspaper. A young guy was starting a computer manufacturing company in Austin, Texas, and needed someone to help him with computer sales in the Southeast. I sent in an application and received an offer to help the young guy generate sales. I had no idea who Michael Dell was, but from his name, now you know the rest of the story.

There are no coincidences, and every person and event that showed up in my life was "meant to be." I listened to many Fortune 500 clients and helped them come up with solutions to their computer needs. Remember, listening to customers will work miracles.

During my journey, I divorced my first husband and eventually met my second husband. Ironically, he happens to be a technical guru. When you're living your purpose, the people, places, and even husbands (clues) show up when they're supposed to. Together we built a beautiful home on a private beach in Florida. We wake up every day to crashing waves and take extensive walks on the beach.

STRONGER SENSE OF SELF

Having self-confidence roots you in who you truly are. You'll be able to accept both your strengths and your weaknesses, knowing that they have nothing to do with your self-worth. Your actions start becoming aligned with your core principles, giving you a greater sense of purpose. You'll know who you are and will have the skills to show up, stand up, and speak up.

INCREASED LEVELS OF MOTIVATION

As you begin to build your self-confidence, you'll be taking small, consistent, daily steps that will leave a lasting sense of accomplishment. If you've ever mastered a language, skill, sport, or fitness goal to get where you wanted to be, you're well on your way already. If you look back at previous achievements, you'll find a common denominator. It will take willingness and determination combined with persistence to achieve your desires. You can't give up. Though it is truly easier said than done, building your self-confidence will bring you one step closer to finding your treasure.

It is helpful to take some time to reflect on the milestones that you've already achieved. For example, think about positive memories, experiences, and personal accomplishments. Even better, write them down and spend time in reflection. This will allow your confidence to grow, and you'll find yourself more driven to achieve bigger goals. With the self-assurance from other achievements, you'll no longer be paralyzed with fear like you once were.

LESS FEAR AND ANXIETY

The more confident you become, the more you'll be able to calm the inner voice that says, "I can't do this." Just being aware of the inner voice is the first step. After becoming aware, you'll be able to detach yourself from these thoughts and start to take action.

If you've found yourself struggling with self-confidence, you're probably familiar with rumination, the tendency to obsess over worries and previous mistakes, replaying them over and over like a broken record.

These tendencies lead to more anxiety and fear in our lives, creating more self-doubt and worry and less confidence. Instead of allowing these continued thoughts, it's important to become aware of what you're thinking and learn how to replace those thoughts with something more productive, thus eliminating the fear and anxiety and replacing it with confidence.

CLUE

The best way to capture moments
is to pay attention. This is how
we cultivate mindfulness.

EXERCISE
Self-Confidence Test

How self-confident are you?

If you had all the confidence in the world, what would you do? Take a moment and write down the first thing that comes to mind. My guess is that there's something you want, but self-doubt and insecurity are holding you back. So let's change that!

Before we move into the four key strategies to improve self-confidence, let's determine where you currently reside with your own self-confidence.

Read each statement in the following list and highlight A if it is true for you most of the time, B if it is true some of the time, and C if it's not usually true.

- I know what my strengths and weaknesses are.   A B C
- I plan and prepare for new experiences.   A B C
- I am willing to take risks.   A B C
- I have faith that things will always work out.   A B C
- I know that God is looking out for me.   A B C
- I take time to write out and remember my achievements and successes.   A B C
- I cope well with unexpected changes.   A B C
- I realize not everyone will like me.   A B C
- I am comfortable asking others for help or support.   A B C
- I know what I value in life.   A B C
- My actions line up with my values.   A B C
- I don't give up easily.   A B C
- I have a strong sense of my worth.   A B C
- I understand that setbacks are a normal part of life.   A B C

- I don't beat myself up when I am going
  through a rough time.   A B C

- I don't allow my thoughts to paralyze me
  when I am attempting to try something new.   A B C

- If I want something badly enough, I know
  I can achieve it.   A B C

To interpret your score, count the total number of As, Bs, and Cs.

Mostly As: You're doing amazing already, not allowing obstacles to get in your way of meeting valued goals. You can learn new skills to improve your self-confidence even more. Congratulations, you're well on your way.

Mostly Bs: You're right smack in the middle. You're able to recognize your accomplishments but sometimes focus on where you're falling short. Your answers indicate that you're subject to feeling as though you've failed, with some common pitfalls that undermine your self-confidence.

Mostly Cs: Your self-confidence needs some work, but that's okay. Remember, no one has self-confidence all of the time, and that's why you're here. Don't be discouraged—you're already on the right track by being honest and recognizing where you fall short. Soon you'll begin to ease up on yourself, take note of your accomplishments, and find manageable ways to handle setbacks. You'll learn how to set goals that are meaningful to you and how to accomplish your goals, all while learning how to cope with any underlying fear or anxiety.

At this stage, you should have a basic understanding of what self-confidence is, why it's important, and where you fall on the self-confidence scale.

Let's take a moment and hear from Maria. She has mastered the art of what it means to be a self-confident woman. She has had a love of fashion and hair design from an early age. She knew what her strengths were, faced her fears head on, and listened to the clues surrounding her.

CLUE

"Sometimes a dream almost whispers...It never shouts. Very hard to hear, so you have to, every day of your lives, be ready to hear what whispers in your ear."

—STEVEN SPIELBERG

Maria A. Barfield
HAIR DESIGN ENTREPRENEUR

Born in Colombia, I immigrated to this beautiful country twenty years ago. I left behind my normal life in pursuit of dreams, goals, and a desire to create a better life for me and my family. However, at the time, I wasn't sure what "better" meant or what my purpose in life was. I had no idea what I should do to start working toward that purpose so that I could ultimately create a happy family.

Having been fascinated by fashion and beauty since the age of five, I made the decision to start a career as a hair stylist. As a child, I loved styling my dolls' hair, which eventually led to styling the hair of all my family members. I remember feeling great joy when I saw their reactions to what I had created. These fond memories were all clues that led me toward my life purpose.

Once I started styling hair professionally, I experienced that same joyful feeling that I had as a child. I recognized that every hairstyle, cut, and color was unique, and nothing about being a stylist was monotonous. I loved watching my clients' reactions when I finished styling their hair. It's what makes my heart sing and provides me with that inner knowing that I am living my life purpose. As the years went by, I started looking for ways to improve my own products to better service my clients.

TREASURE HUNT RULE
*Pay attention to how
things make you feel.*

The gift from the divine is to be honored and shared. My passion for creating hair designs was inspired by my grandmother. After she passed, I heard a faint whisper from her while I was sleeping. She motivated me to create hair care products from nature that strengthen your hair, leaving it silky and healthy.

It was at this moment that she provided me with her natural recipe for several hair care products. After that magical night, I began to create shampoo, conditioner, and hair growth formulas. I tested them on myself, family, and eventually my clients. The more I improved the products, the more my clients loved them.

When I'm finished styling my clients' hair, they use words to describe their hair like *silky, smooth, shiny,* and *healthy.* They notice right away that something is significantly different about my products and want to know the ingredients. They're even more excited to learn that everything I use is organic and natural.

I recognized that finding your life purpose is finding an opportunity that you're passionate about and that provides a solution to an existing problem. It must be a solution that is new, unique, and that people really desire and need. All my clients tell me that my hair care products are the best that they've ever used.

As a single mother raising a son and a daughter, I realize what my mother went through to raise my brother and I. She made great sacrifices to bring us to the United States. I remember vividly every time she told me the importance of coming to the US to make a better life for her kids so that we could make a better life for ours. She emphasized the importance of having a happy and peaceful life. For me, to be happy you must find something you love doing, find ways to help as many people as you can, and be at peace with your family, friends, and your God.

It can be tough at times, and you may face fear, doubt, and lack of self-confidence. That's why it's always better to reach out for help and be aware that sometimes help comes to you. For example, I had the good fortune of having a mother who sacrificed her own dreams for others. She thought about what was best for her kids in the long term and convinced us to come to the US. She taught me the importance of having a dream and going after it relentlessly.

Luckily, I met Melissa and Rita, two of my clients who motivated me to commercialize my products and who put me in contact with people who knew how to do it. I am extremely grateful for their support. They represent, along with my mother and grandmother, how powerful women can help other women be successful. I consider these women my angels, who guide me in pursuit of my purpose. They have been additional clues toward finding my life's purpose.

In the middle of the pandemic I opened my own studio and sold my own brand of shampoo and conditioners. I realize that I'm making more people happier by making their hair look silky smooth, shinier, and healthier by using natural ingredients whispered to me by the most influential woman in my life, my grandmother. In return, I am happier and now have more time to devote to my son, daughter, and grandkids.

I will leave you with this critical lesson: women can be more powerful when they help other people. I will forever be grateful for my mother and grandmother, powerful women who taught me that in life it's not enough to have a dream and a purpose. You must fight for your right to be happy. Fear is nothing more than a trigger to do something to get you closer to your goals. When we begin to sense fear or doubt, that's when women can help the most.

As someone who moved from fear and lack of confidence to how I feel today, let me offer this to you: come to my studio in Fort Lauderdale, Florida, try my products, and if you don't walk out thinking this is the best my hair has ever looked, it's on me.

For booking or more information about my products, visit mariabarfield.glossgenius.com.

C L U E

"Do we meet people by accident?
I am not so sure. Our paths
cross for a reason and it is up to
us to search for the WHY."

—LAWRENCE JONES, MBE

The Three Key Strategies for Developing Self-Confidence and Sustaining Self-Love

Now that you're on your personal journey to achieving your God-given life purpose, let's examine the three key strategies that will help every woman to develop more self-confidence and sustaining self-love. Each of these strategies is important, but when mastered together, they will create an unstoppable and lasting foundation:

- Developing uncommon faith
- Facing your fears
- Becoming aware of negative self-talk and developing new core beliefs

DEVELOPING UNCOMMON FAITH

If you want to master self-confidence, develop a level of faith that is unbreakable. For different people, having faith may be linked to God, a universal force, or a spiritual entity. For me and for purposes of this example, it's God. Take the time to look away from all of the outside distractions and focus on your God. When you're facing tests in your life, a lot of things will try to draw your attention away from your faith. God wants us to keep our eyes on him and not allow these distractions to bring us down.

It's easy to run to the outside world when problems arise. We search on the internet, call friends and family, and become distracted by binge-watching our favorite shows. To truly live a life of uncommon faith means that you turn to God and place him first when you're facing any and all life challenges. Ask yourself, "What does God think about this situation?" This should be the final word. The stronger you build your faith, the more able you are to face and tackle any potential obstacle that comes your way. The more faith you build, the deeper your self-confidence becomes.

It took me years to develop unshakable amounts of faith. I still struggle sometimes. However, as I have gone through more life experiences and started to find answers to some of my earlier life events, various pieces of the puzzle have come together and now make perfect sense. This is why it is important to recognize various clues that occur in your life's journey. Be sure to write these clues down and keep an ongoing clue journal. It's easy to look back and connect the dots, but it takes talent to proactively become aware as clues occur. It takes even greater awareness to understand how the clues can come together in perfect harmony.

Once you have achieved this status, we shall crown you a clue connector. These types of aha moments have led me in my personal development of unbreakable faith. It doesn't mean that I'm not scared sometimes, or that my old ways of doubt and worry don't creep in. This is normal and will happen from time to time.

It's important to have consistent faith. The word of God should be at the tip of your tongue during times of rejoicing and in times of challenges. As you develop your faith, you learn to speak boldly over any situation and have the confidence that things are being handled for the greater good.

It's really no secret that prayer builds our faith. Learn to pray with your heart. Your heart is where faith is produced. All the forces of life flow through your heart. Make sure to continually give God praise. Don't wait until things have manifested in their physical form before giving praise to God. Get in the habit of thanking God every day for things that you desire that still haven't come to fruition. This type of faith will assist you in developing sustaining self-confidence.

Melissa Butterworth

CEO, ENTREPRENEUR

MY FIFTH CLUE: FLASHBACK

October 2017, Miami, Florida

The real aha moment that led me to have uncommon faith occurred five years ago. I went through a decade of my life trying to get answers for some earlier circumstances that were unpleasant. Instead of leaving the answers up to God, I insisted on trying to figure out the answers myself.

Earlier, I shared my story about having been fired during my early thirties. I spent over ten years fighting a legal battle against a billion-dollar corporation to get what I thought was rightfully owed to me. I thought that the battle was mine to take on, when in reality it was always in God's hands. He saw that I had been wronged and was about to pay me back tenfold for the wrongdoings. It just wasn't in "my timing" and wasn't the way I expected.

I would end up losing the ten-year lawsuit and, through the process, my financial fortune. However, the same month that the lawsuit concluded, I did a business deal with that same company, and the total sales commissions came out to the *exact* dollar amount that I claimed the company owed me, plus all of the legal fees that I had incurred. I was profoundly shocked and left speechless.

This outcome left me with a knowing that there is a much higher power in the works. This is when my faith was catapulted to an entirely different level. It was my moment of insight. From that moment forward, I have developed uncommon faith. And I've had many other aha moments since then. I am now keenly aware and therefore understand their deeper spiritual meaning. Of course, there are many events that have happened that I still have no answers for. It is through these events that my faith can still be tested from time to time.

What could that decade of my life have looked like if I had developed uncommon amounts of faith earlier in life? What if I had developed uncommon faith before trying to take matters into my own hands? Perhaps it took this extraordinary situation for me to wake up and realize that God handles our battles for us, and, on his timetable. Let my story be a valuable lesson for you.

> ### TREASURE HUNT RULE
> *Sometimes a big clue
> requires no explanation.*

FACING YOUR FEARS

It's human nature to experience fear and anxiety. When you believe in yourself, you realize that those emotions are there to encourage you to take action, not to hold you back. The most common fears are these:

- Rejection
- Failure and/or success
- Love or lack of love
- Being alone
- The unknown
- Death

Are you currently struggling with any of these fears? They can infiltrate our thinking and our opinion of ourselves. These fears have a tendency to paralyze us if we allow them to. At the end of this chapter, we encourage you to take the Facing Your Fears Challenge. This will help you overcome any fear that you may have.

Face your fears by creating goals that are connected to your overall purpose in life. Setting and achieving goals that help you overcome your fears will give you a sense of accomplishment. Your goals don't have to be huge; taking small steps that add up to big results will improve your confidence and boost your faith in yourself.

Let's look at how Christal managed to successfully overcome what could have been perceived as rejection in her career. She faced these challenges head on by being brave and has achieved partnership status by the age of forty.

Christal Contini

PARTNER-LAWYER, MCDONALD HOPKINS

I am a woman, and I can swear like a sailor (of course, not all the time). I was ten when my aunt Marie explained to me that there is a time and a place for most things in life, including four-letter words. So, the truth is, I didn't learn to sling slang while working in the trenches as a mergers and acquisitions lawyer. It has nothing to do with the fact that I work primarily with men. No, this is a skill I have honed over a lifetime, and it started with my father.

My father is 100 percent Italian, retired after working over forty years at a factory, and was the secretary of his union. If he does anything, he does it with passion. He taught me that I could be anything, but whatever I chose, I needed to be the best at it. He showed his passion every day in his work, raising two confident women, running, grilling, and yes, "communicating."

I remember being sixteen and backing my POS powder blue Dodge Aries into his recently washed and waxed pristine white 1969 Lincoln Town Car. The sound of metal on metal was deafening, but it paled in comparison to my father's tirade of profanity. If I hadn't been so scared of his wrath, I would have been impressed by his creativity.

My mother, on the other hand, is a supreme diplomat. She has this uncanny ability to defuse drama, build consensus, and simply bring out the good in people. She brokered my return to the house after the car crash, and she winked and told me that she "hated that car anyway." My father still loves me.

Given this background, it should not surprise anyone that I became an M&A lawyer. My job is to be a professional communicator and to build consensus. I was drawn to this area of law because I get to help people achieve significant life and career goals. For example, I often represent sellers who have built a successful business over a lifetime. I advocate for their interests when selling their business to the next steward of growth so that they can enjoy retirement or invest in a new opportunity. This transition is a time when people are incredibly vulnerable, and, as you can imagine, it's a time that can sometimes lead to heated moments and "creative" communication.

People often refer to doing due diligence on a company as "peeking under a woman's dress," and to difficult negotiations as one party having to "bend over." I love metaphors as much as the next girl, but where are my car fans? I think "looking under the hood of the car" as a due diligence metaphor would suffice!

While I faced many obstacles being a woman in M&A, four-letter words had not been one of them. In my first year as a partner at my firm, I had the opportunity to pitch with one of my male colleagues (let's call him Dave), representing a distribution company out of San Francisco in its sale to a strategic acquirer. I spent hours preparing for the meeting, bought a new dress, had my nails done, and got my hair cut and colored. I was ready. (Nothing against Dave, but I'm sure his biggest stressor was choosing which pants to pack.)

This was a bid process, and we knew that a competing law firm had already pitched to the company the day before. We met with two men: the company's chief executive officer and the chief financial officer. I was admittedly nervous at the beginning, but Dave expertly moved us from a presentation to a conversation. I left that office knowing that we rocked the pitch!

On our way to the airport, we talked about the meeting highlights. I noted that the CEO with the bright pink pocket square liked to direct his questions to Dave, even though I was clearly the one who had the expertise and would answer the questions. Dave noticed it, too, but we both agreed that the CEO seemed to get more comfortable with me as the discussion progressed.

The next day Dave heard from one of the decision-makers, and to his credit, he gave us the real story. Unfortunately, we didn't win the work. The executives thought we presented well and gave great answers, and they asked the competing law firm to beat our price quote. Unfortunately, the CEO did not select our law firm because he "didn't feel comfortable swearing in front of a lady." Seriously? I could not decide which angered me more—the gender bias or that, being my father's daughter, I could easily win a cussing contest if put to the test.

I was incredibly discouraged after that rejection by Mr. Pink Pocket Square, and I doubted my ability to become a lead attorney and business generator at my law firm. However, I kept doing the job I loved, I expanded my expertise in growing industries, and I set out to find opportunities to work with like-minded professionals.

One such professional I was lucky enough to encounter was Melissa Butterworth, the author of this inspiring book. We have referred clients to each other, presented at conferences together, and closed transactions together. I have learned the importance of working with professionals who share my business philosophy, work ethic, and focus on client service. Through this approach, I have significantly grown my practice, and today I am the chair of the mergers and acquisitions practice group at McDonald Hopkins LLC.

As I continue to grow as a lawyer and leader at my firm, I try to encourage young attorneys from all different backgrounds to find their unique practice niche, communication style, and people they want to build a career with. I choose to ignore the Mr. Pink Pocket Squares of the world, and I'm sure you can all imagine where my dad would tell that guy to shove his pocket square. I hope all our clients see what I see: that female lawyers are talented, detail-oriented, and fierce negotiators. We are your advocates, and we know how to build consensus in an ever-changing business landscape. And yes, most of us swear.

BECOMING AWARE OF NEGATIVE SELF-TALK AND DEVELOPING NEW CORE BELIEFS

Many people battle negative thinking every day. We can find ourselves obsessing over the reasons we can't do something or aren't good enough, working ourselves into a frenzy until it greatly affects our performance. Our negative thinking eventually becomes a self-fulfilling prophecy, lowering our self-confidence and keeping us from achieving our potential.

Have you ever caught yourself saying any of the following statements in silence or out loud?

- There's no way they would like me.
- I'm such a loser.
- How could I ever get into that school?
- I'm not smart enough.
- I wish I was prettier.
- I'm always late.
- How could I ever have my own business?
- I'm so stupid.
- Gosh, I look fat in that.
- I'm not good enough.
- I can't get anything right.

- · I am weak.

- · I'm all alone.

- · My needs don't matter.

All of us have a near-constant stream of thoughts running through our minds. Most of the time these thoughts are neutral, and sometimes they're even pleasant. However, the thoughts that cause our self-confidence to dwindle are the automatic negative ones—otherwise known as *cognitive distortions*. These are the thoughts that don't serve us well.

It isn't the negative thoughts themselves that are the issue—it's the power that we give the thoughts. But we don't have to give them power. Once we recognize these negative thoughts, we can choose to believe them, or we can choose to disregard them.

To help you recognize these negative thoughts, let's give them categories.

ALL-OR-NOTHING THINKING

The all-or-nothing mentality, otherwise known as perfectionism, sets most people up for failure no matter what. For example, saying to yourself, "If I don't get into the university of my dreams, I will never be a success," is an all-or-nothing statement.

This type of thinking is shortsighted. There is a lot of beauty and opportunity between the lines of perfectionism and doubt, where a lot of people end up. There are skills you gain along the way. You gain confidence from taking steps toward your goals. And you develop a sense of pride in knowing that you went for your goals. Sure, there may be mistakes made along the journey, but this is how we learn.

MAKING ASSUMPTIONS: FEELINGS VS. FACTS

It's important to know when you're allowing your feelings to spin your life's narrative into something negative. For example, using the previous example, you could make assumptions that you didn't get accepted into the college of your dreams because you're not smart enough.

Many people make assumptions without having any specific evidence to back them up. When you make assumptions, you're essentially filling the void of the unknown by imagining an undesirable outcome. You start allowing your emotions to get the best of you. If you're not careful, this can lead to self-sabotage and possibly ruin the gift that you are about to receive.

Meanwhile, there are a million other possible reasons that you haven't heard anything. Perhaps the mail is slow, or maybe the college extended their deadlines. There are many good options that are possible, yet we have gotten into a habit of making negative assumptions. The key is to recognize when you're making assumptions, write them down, and learn to replace those thoughts with something positive. Recognize that feelings are not facts.

SHOULDING

If you've gotten into a routine of focusing on where you *should* be in life, or what you *should* be doing, you're engaging in "shoulding." Essentially, you're setting inflexible standards for yourself that you've already failed to meet. This type of perfectionism is rough on your self-confidence. For example, I spent a lot of my twenties comparing myself to friends of the same age.

I was hard on myself because most of my friends were already married and having their first child. They didn't have the same level of career success that I did (I was married to my job), but they were far ahead of me in their personal lives. I was worried that I *should* have already found the perfect mate, and I found myself lonely at times. This type of comparison and "shoulding" only caused me more loneliness in the long run.

EXERCISE
Becoming Aware of Negative Self-Talk

Here are two exercises to help you become aware of your negative self-talk.

Think about three goals that you would like to achieve this year. Start thinking about the process of pursuing each goal. List any negative thoughts that come to mind. Then, identify which category each thought fits into.

Carry a journal with you for the next week and use it to keep an inventory of which types of automatic negative thoughts pop into your mind—all or nothing, assumptions, or "shoulding."

Answer the following questions:

- What are you telling yourself?
- What do you fear will happen?
- Which area of my life are these negative thoughts focused on?

The key to this exercise is to start becoming aware of what you're telling yourself, where it's coming from, and what you're most afraid of. Patterns will likely emerge.

THE FIVE STEPS TO BREAKING NEGATIVE THOUGHT PATTERNS

Once you've become aware of your thought patterns, the key is to break the negative ones once and for all. The following five steps will assist you with this.

1. **Identify your distortions**. Review your journal and notice which cognitive distortions you seem to fall prey to. For example, are you one of those people who falls into the comparison trap or is constantly "shoulding"? Or are you the type of person who draws quick assumptions without looking at all the facts first? Identifying where your weaknesses are will help you break the cycle.

2. **Challenge your thinking.** As you write down the thoughts that pop up during the week and their corresponding distortions, start challenging

these thoughts and ask yourself, Is this really true? Have I checked the facts? Do I know this for certain? Take a step back and challenge your thinking. Continue challenging and pose the question: Am I really a bad person, or was I simply doing the best I knew how to at the time?

3. **Have compassionate self-talk.** We are our own worst enemy. We can be harsh, negative, and outright abusive to ourselves at times. For each distortion you've identified throughout the week, ask yourself, Would I ever speak to a friend like this? For example, if you find yourself constantly telling yourself that you're fat, ask yourself, Would I call my friend fat? Hopefully not. Now practice being more compassionate with yourself.

4. **Seek support.** Find a friend you trust who can help you identify and challenge the assumptions and distortions that you've identified about yourself. The people who you spend the most time with might have valuable feedback about how they see you talking to yourself. They might notice changes to your body language, personality, emotions, and so on.

5. **Assess the positive and negative outcomes.** True self-assessment is key to finding the mental and emotional freedom you're looking for as you begin to challenge your specific cognitive distortions. By assessing the positive and negative outcomes of your thought patterns, you can decide if it's worth making a change. Answer the following questions:

   - How will it help or hurt you if you continue to believe this distortion?
   - How do you feel about yourself when you talk to yourself this way?
   - Does believing this distortion help or harm your self-confidence?

In summary, learn which cognitive distortions you've been telling yourself. Keep a journal and start to challenge these types of negative self-talk. It does take a lot of practice and patience, but your life will become better as you learn to control your thoughts instead of letting them control you. You will begin to notice a significant improvement in your self-confidence.

EXERCISE
Facing Your Fears Challenge

Do you find yourself holding back in life because of the fears that fill your head with self-doubt? Remember that fear is a natural part of our evolutionary heritage. It's important to have a fear response mechanism so that we don't run a traffic light or try to touch a hot stove. Exposure is the best way to tackle our fears. The more you expose yourself to something you fear, the less it will be a big deal to you. Take out your journal and complete the following:

1. Make a list of the things that you currently fear. For example, you might have a fear of speaking in public, driving, taking timed tests, asking a friend out on a date, moving away to college, or flying. Write out anything that comes to mind, and don't be judgmental of yourself.

2. Rate the stress or anxiety (on a scale from 1 to 10) you think you would experience as a result of facing each of these fears (with 10 being the worst possible stress or anxiety).

3. For each item you fear, create a plan of action to overcome that fear. For example, if you fear public speaking, your list might include the following steps:

    · Go to YouTube and search for TED Talks. Spend twenty minutes watching speakers.

    · Prepare a one-minute speech about yourself.

    · Stand in front of the mirror and practice your speech.

    · Ask your parents if you can practice your one-minute speech in front of them.

    · Ask your best friend if you can practice speaking in front of them.

    · Join a local speaking club such as Toastmasters and start speaking regularly.

4. Complete a plan for each item that you currently fear.

CLUE

"Stay afraid, but do it anyway. What's important is the action. You don't have to wait to be confident, just do it and eventually the confidence will follow."

—CARRIE FISHER

EXERCISE
15 Self-Confidence Boosters

Take out your journal and write down these 15 practices to help boost your sense of confidence personally and professionally. Start practicing them today.

1. **Smile more.** Even if you feel nervous, the act of smiling can help make you feel comfortable and improve your mood. Smiling serves as an example of positive body language, encouraging other people to interact with you. Smiling while giving a presentation or feedback can help your audience perceive you as a confident individual, so they'll trust what you say. The key is to smile more to boost your own confidence level.

2. **Project a confident appearance.** When you feel confident about how you look, it can encourage confidence in other aspects of your life. For example, wearing an outfit that makes you feel comfortable and powerful can help ease your nerves during a job interview. You can use this technique as a method of self-care, such as getting a manicure or facial. Beyond providing more confidence in your outward appearance, these tactics can help you feel more relaxed. When you feel your best, you project a more confident image.

3. **Keep a compliment journal.** Begin your day by writing yourself some compliments. These compliments can focus on both professional and personal traits and skills. For example, you may express appreciation for how well dressed you are in addition to your willingness to help others at work. This tactic allows you to focus on your positive aspects rather than on your insecurities. You can document some of the compliments that others have recently given you. Documenting these compliments in a journal enables you to return to them when you feel less confident.

4. **Celebrate your wins.** Focusing on the positive events in your life can help you maintain confidence. For example, if you begin a new habit or achieve a personal goal, consider rewarding yourself. Recognizing these successes can help you feel confident about your abilities and give you motivation for future achievements.

5. **Think about your skills.** Another way to focus on your positive attributes is to think about the skills you possess. You can do this exercise alone or ask family members, friends, or colleagues for their insights. Reflecting on these skills can help remind you of what makes you a talented person or an effective employee. Once you identify these skills, you can focus on using and highlighting them at work to showcase your strengths.

6. **Reflect on your past achievements.** Create a list of some of your proudest achievements to remind you of your successes. These achievements can be both personal and professional. For example, you may mention events like earning a medal in a race or getting accepted to college. You can list results-related achievements, such as increasing your organization's revenue. When you think about these prior successes, it can give you confidence in your skills and abilities. You can use this confidence to motivate yourself toward more achievements.

7. **Practice meditation.** Meditation allows you to control your thoughts and can help you build your confidence. Through mindfulness practice, you can learn how to observe your thoughts without judgment. You can visualize yourself accomplishing tasks and being successful. This anxiety-reducing practice helps you fix your thoughts in the present moment and improve your mental well-being.

8. **Share your opinions.** You can practice being outspoken and confident by sharing your opinions more often. For example, you may speak up and explain your ideas for an upcoming project during class. The more you practice these habits, the more comfortable you'll feel performing them over time. Sharing these thoughts can help you feel like your ideas matter and that others hear you.

9. **Maintain a healthy body image.** Maintaining your physical well-being can help you feel more confident. When you feel good, it shows in your mood, behaviors, and appearance. Healthy food and exercise habits can reduce feelings of stress, allowing you to feel ready to take on your responsibilities with confidence.

   I don't know a single woman who hasn't gotten caught up in the vicious cycle of trying to maintain the perfect body. It's an unfortunate trap fueled by outside factors that have existed for centuries. The key is to develop healthy habits early in life to avoid falling into a lifelong trap of fad diets that do nothing but mess with our metabolisms.

   I have personally found the best program to learn about lifelong health and nutritional habits is OPTAVIA, created by Dr. Wayne Scott Andersen. You can learn more about this program through his book, *Dr. A's Habits of Health*. I love it because it was written by a well-respected doctor, is based on science, and has helped hundreds of millions of people understand how to eat properly to maintain a healthy body mass index. I can personally speak about this program, having lost thirty-two pounds on OPTAVIA while writing this book.

10. **Do a power pose.** As mentioned, positive body language can influence how you perceive yourself. Using a power pose in private can help boost your mood and confidence when you feel nervous or uncomfortable. For example, you may try using this technique before entering a job interview or making a presentation at work. A typical power pose involves standing with your hands on your hips and your legs shoulder-width apart.

11. **Give yourself a powerful alter ego.** When working on an assignment, think about how someone you respect would approach the task. You can create an alter ego that combines the qualities of your expert coworkers or a fictitious character you admire. Taking on this persona can help separate you from your thoughts and feelings of self-consciousness. Getting into character as this confident individual with expert knowledge can help you feel more comfortable perceiving yourself this way.

12. **Create a self-esteem collage.** A self-esteem collage can serve as a visual reminder of your value. This collage may be similar to your treasure map but is meant to be focused on areas that have impacted your self-confidence. For example, you may have had a negative experience with speaking in public. In your self-esteem collage, you can put a picture of yourself on a stage looking out into a large audience.

    Place this collage somewhere you'll see it daily to give yourself a regular boost. When putting together this collage, include images that represent your positive attributes. Every time you look at those images, you'll think about what makes you great or unique. You may want to incorporate images that represent your personal or professional aspirations. As a result, the collage can help serve as a reminder and motivational tool for working toward those goals.

13. **Listen to music.** Listening to high-energy music can help influence your mood when you need a boost of confidence. The music that motivates you may vary depending on your interests. For example, rock music with heavy bass can help pump up some people's excitement levels or make them feel powerful. You may consider music that makes you dance to shake out any nervous energy you have. Whatever genre you choose, make sure that it leaves you feeling happy, energized, and ready to take on any situation.

14. **Join a club or take up a sport or hobby.** Typically, when we engage in an activity that we're good at, we learn how to develop more confidence. Confidence is something developed through focus, effort, and repetition. It's best to identify what you love to do. For example, if you love to dance, look into starting dance classes. If you love to play tennis, join a local tennis club.

Hundreds of clubs and classes can help develop certain skills, such as cooking, writing, computers, arts, drama, knitting, and more. The key is to get involved in something outside of school or work that further ignites what you're passionate about. If you wish to become more spiritual, start attending church. If you fear public speaking, join a speaking organization such as Toastmasters and learn to become the best speaker possible. (This is something I recommend to everyone reading this book. Learning to become an effective speaker is an ideal way to improve your self-confidence, excel in any profession, and set yourself apart from your peers.)

15. **Find a mentor.** One of the best ways to develop more self-confidence is to find a mentor. Mentoring is a relationship between two people with the goal of professional and personal development. The mentor is usually an experienced individual who shares their experience and advice with a less experienced person, or mentee. The mentors become trusted advisers and role models—people who have "been there and done that." They support and encourage their mentees by offering suggestions and knowledge, both general and specific. The goal is to help the mentees improve their skills, which will subsequently help boost self-confidence.

Once you've uncovered your life purpose, God will place certain people in your path who will become possible mentors at different times throughout your life. It will become your job to recognize these people, embrace them, and follow the path put in front of you. As you learned in Maria's story, God placed several powerful women (clues) in her path. It was through these women that she has turned her dream into a reality.

It's never too late in life to reinvent yourself. Let's look at how Cheryl was able to start a new and thriving business by recognizing one of the clues that came into her life through mentorship.

CLUE

The Universe is within you—
bright and beautiful.

Cheryl Adelman

ENTREPRENEUR, ORGANIZE IN A DAY

I started my home organizing business, Organize in a Day™, at the age of fifty-nine. I enthusiastically and gratefully celebrated six years in business in April 2022. The name of my business was my mentor's idea, one of her many gifts to me. I started this business late in life, but the timing was perfect for me.

I owned two previous businesses that didn't achieve financial success. I did, however, learn. My husband and I started a small catering business, a clean and upscale lunch truck called Food Dude. I designed a legal commercial kitchen to be built in our home, oversaw the process to legally zone the kitchen and operation of the business, and ran everything from there. I learned that street smarts can take you far, but success in business comes down to relationships.

However, after years of working too hard with little reward, I needed to leave the business, and my husband. I decided to complete my college degree.

Next, I became an independent, self-employed massage therapist in South Jersey, then South Florida, a beautiful career lasting fifteen years. I enjoyed having loyal clients, and I identified strongly with this work. But I was still just eking out a living. I knew there was more to life.

Meanwhile, I raised my wonderful daughter. The parenting journey is imperfect, yet the rewards are vast, much like being an entrepreneur.

Then—BAM!—came the life-changing event at age fifty-eight. I met the woman (clue) who became my dear friend, inspired me to start my own business, step into my power, and have a better life. She also became my business mentor. She is a successful entrepreneur, intelligent, strategic, generous with information, experienced, and kind. Having her support and encouragement has been invaluable. She continues to share business insights and her keen understanding of human nature with me.

I am so fortunate. I could not have made it without her advice and guidance, and, as a result, my life changed for the better. And knowing her is such a joy. She calls her work with me "love in action." She has been one of life's major clues to helping me find my purpose. Since starting this work, I have been steadily stepping into my power as an entrepreneur and as a person.

I had no idea how to "rise and shine," until I embraced her advice to "Keep going!" She helps me see the best in myself.

Today, I know my work brings value to people's lives, and I keep growing.

Over 200 five-star reviews validate that I'm in the right business: enhancing and transforming homes and lives. And as an entrepreneur, I can maintain my integrity and independence and continue making my own choices while being in service to others. I know I'm incredibly fortunate to be running my own small business and taking care of myself, especially with the economic disruption happening now.

As owner and sole proprietor of Organize in a Day—my home organizing and moving preparation business—I do sales, marketing, customer relations, and branding, as well as the work of organizing and moving preparation. I'm learning to reach out to other experts when it's smart to trust someone else more skilled and better suited than I for certain tasks. Being financially independent now for the first time in my life is empowering. I wish the same for every woman. May we all make decisions thoughtfully, holding our personal and financial freedom as the beacon.

And now, I am inspired to say, "I want more!"

I am examining and exploring what the next iteration of this business can be.

I continue to find my way by taking deliberate action (an expression my mentor taught me), becoming an expert in my field, being in service, and being sincerely grateful.

Side note: My entrepreneurial lineage started in a small town (Shtetl) on the outskirts of Kiev, Ukraine, whence my grandfather left for America. He went from being a door-to-door peddler to having three storefronts in a row selling furniture on a major commercial street in northeast Philadelphia. In short, he was an entrepreneur. His entrepreneurial drive may have been rooted in desperation, but he combined it with a fierce courage that was likely not recognized until looking back.

Two of his three sons became entrepreneurs, one daughter married one, and the other daughter, my mother, loved working in her father's store. I inherited the entrepreneurial gene.

Follow the Clues

- Step 6 of your personal journey toward your God-given life purpose is to develop sustaining self-confidence. The three key strategies to enhance your self-confidence are

    1. Developing uncommon faith,

    2. Facing your fears, and

    3. Becoming aware of negative self-talk and developing new core beliefs.

- Self-confidence is self-discovery—finding out who you are and what you're truly capable of accomplishing.

- Each one of us has a continuous inner dialogue throughout the day. We talk more to ourselves than anyone. Pay attention to how you talk to yourself. Once you learn how to talk to yourself in the right way, you'll rise to a new level of self-confidence.
- Take the self-confidence quiz to understand how confident you currently are.
- Learn how to overcome your fears by taking the Face Your Fears Challenge included in this chapter.

PART III

8

THE REAL TREASURE

Step 7: Discover Your Strengths, Talents, Vision, and Purpose

Congratulations. You now have an understanding of the bigger picture or the 12 stages of the Hero's Journey. You have identified what stage of the journey you may have been stuck in and are able to proceed forward with the knowledge of where you are headed and desire to be. You have started to implement the five steps mentioned in previous chapters so you can build a lifelong sustainable foundation. You are acutely aware of the clues that have been occurring in your own life. It's time to dig further and do the exercises that will help you in uncovering your purpose.

This chapter will lead you toward the ultimate treasure you have been looking for. It's time to discover your strengths, talents, vision, and ultimate purpose in life. You have all of the tools to withstand any and all challenges that you may face in life.

Before you were born, God (or your chosen higher power) envisioned you and provided you with gifts and talents that are unique to you. He blessed you with creativity and ideas, as well as areas in which you can excel in life. If we are not moving toward our life purpose, dissatisfaction and tension will always exist in our inner being. The major reason that so many people are unhappy, restless, and lacking enthusiasm is that they aren't fulfilling their destiny. My desire for you is that you'll follow God's divine destiny for your life, uncover your individual strengths and talents, discover your calling, and stay in your purpose.

It's time to dig deeper and understand why you're on this planet. Like a treasure hunt, one must dig deep to find the gold within. Life doesn't come with an instruction manual, so identifying our life purpose can be a challenge. Some people go through their entire life and never figure out what their purpose is. Others seem to discover their life purpose at a very young age. How can some be so fortunate while others simply drift throughout life not being able to determine their God-given purpose?

To get our lives on track and work toward our life purpose, we must clear our minds from all the clutter. Empty your mind of everything, everyone around you, and anything others have told you that you should be doing with your life. Stop comparing yourself to others. We all have different strengths and skill sets and have our own special purpose for being here. If you aren't careful, you could allow the opinions of others to form who you think you should be. It's time to throw out others' preconceived notions of who you are or what you should become.

Some people try to map out and plan their picture-perfect life by setting goals. They make their plans to go to college and get a degree by the time they're twenty-two. They're determined to land the perfect corporate job and meet their perfect spouse. They have dreams to have several kids and live the perfect life. There's nothing wrong with having plans and setting goals, but many times life doesn't work out the way we'd planned, and most of the time your life is not the vision of perfect you had planned for.

There is a higher power, and no matter what your religious beliefs are, the universe has a way of showing us when we're going in the right direction. Things will open up, people will come into your life, and life's magic starts to flow. It's critical to declutter your mind so you can become aware of the clues and unexpected opportunities that will come into your life.

CLUE

"Don't ask yourself what the world
needs. Ask yourself what makes
you come alive, and go do that,
because what the world needs is
people who have come alive."

—HOWARD THURMAN

CLUE

We must be willing to let go of the life we've planned in order to have the life that is waiting for us.

Up until this moment, you may have looked outside yourself, into the world, to be told what your purpose is. You may have thought it was in a relationship, career, job, or person. You were searching externally when the answer could only be found within; hence, the search was taking a long time.

Today, I want you to focus on why you've clung so tightly to all of the old patterns and behaviors you identified in the last chapter—and why it's a great idea to let them go. Your logical brain needs a little time to catch up to your soul. So it's time to find your "why." This will bring you one step closer to discovering your own treasure.

There is so much power in the clarity of knowing why you're here. That's why it's crucial for you to determine your life purpose. Having a life purpose will guide you to living a happy and fulfilled life. When you know your why, it will become your driving force and you'll never give up. This is one of the reasons I love the OPTAVIA plan for weight loss and life maintenance of proper health and nutrition. Dr. Andersen, author of *Dr. A's Habits for Health*, has his clients go through several exercises of which one of them is determining their why for wanting to live a long and healthy life at a healthy weight. Once you uncover your why, the rest becomes easy.

So start thinking—what is the one thing that you want more than anything else in the whole world? I encourage you to think big. If you aren't sure, that's okay. I will take you through several exercises that will help you navigate those uncertain pastures. If you know your life purpose, these exercises will help you further clarify the next steps toward ensuring that you achieve all of your dreams.

In the following section, we'll look at these areas:

- The difference between your vision, purpose, and goals
- The primary and secondary emotions that drive you
- The qualities, strengths, and talents that make you unique
- The events, people, places, and clues that helped shape you into who you are and that may be leading you towards your life purpose
- Why we need to learn to lead with the heart

Identifying your life purpose is a combination of all these factors, and it's important to understand each area.

Understanding the Difference Between Your Vision, Purpose, and Goals

Your **vision** is your hope for what the future could look like. It's essentially your dream of what is possible. For example, it could consist of your thoughts about how you could help others and make the world a better place. Your vision is an answer to an existing problem that needs to be solved and tends to be something that speaks to you more than others. Your vision is outwardly focused and tends to be something much bigger than you, yet it's within your reach with the proper amount of desire, passion, and planning.

For example, when I first started my mergers and acquisitions (M&A) laboratory firm (a company that sells small laboratories to larger ones), my vision was to help lab owners understand the M&A process and how to maximize the value of their business when they decided to sell. I realized that business owners devoted their entire lives to building their companies and could benefit from my specialized knowledge of the laboratory M&A process. I also recognized that while there were several business bankers in the space already, none of them came from the laboratory industry and understood the business from the ground up. This would become the key differentiator that allowed me to excel in my chosen profession.

Your **purpose** is the answer to the biggest question you'll likely have while living on this earth: "What am I here for?" It's something that, when identified, will set your soul on fire. If you don't know what your life purpose is, that's okay. You're in the right spot, and we'll soon get there. The next step is to put yourself in a purpose mindset. That means identifying your personal values, emotions that drive you, and how you are called to make a difference. For example, my life purpose is to use my connections and knowledge to ensure that others reach their fullest potential and create their dream life.

Your **goals** are the stepping-stones that keep you on track as you live purposefully. Achieving a goal on its own is great, but it must have a larger meaning that can be recognized as a stepping-stone toward your larger vision and life purpose. A goal can be checked off a list and accomplished; whereas, one's life purpose is something you'll live out for a long period of time.

You'll know when you've identified your life purpose because it will leave you feeling exhilarated, alive, and full of everlasting energy. You won't be able to stop thinking about it.

CLUE

"Many people are alive but don't
touch the miracle of being alive."

–THICH NHAT HANH

EXERCISE
Uncovering Emotions Related to Memories

To put your life purpose in a better perspective, think of it as an emotion or combination of emotions. Emotion is what creates life. When you can successfully tap into your emotions, you can understand and own the emotions you want to feel, and opportunities will find you.

You'll suddenly find yourself on a path where everything in life magically opens up. Your path will unfold and events that seem like miracles will start to happen. When your life matches the true beat of your soul, everything is possible. Experiencing positive emotions means that you're aligned with your soul. When you feel negative emotions, it's a sign you need to change your limiting beliefs or get aligned with what makes you happy.

1. Take the next ten minutes and apply one of the meditation techniques discussed earlier. Place your hand over your heart and close your eyes as you pay attention to your breathing. If your mind begins to wander, just keep focusing on your breathing. Allow ten to fifteen minutes to pass.

2. When you're in a calm state, answer the following questions:

    - What is the earliest, happiest moment in your life that you can remember? Write down the first memory that comes to mind.

    - Who was with you?

    - What did you believe about life at that time?

3. Repeat the entire exercise until you've come up with at least five happy memories from your life. They don't have to be in chronological order.

While you're completing the questions, allow yourself the time to remember all of the people, places, and experiences and consider the feelings associated with those events. This exercise allows you to use these memories to uncover the emotions that bring you the greatest joy. Our plan is to design a life for you that will encompass the emotions that these favorite memories ignite within you.

The joy that you feel when remembering fond memories is the feeling of being connected to your soul. Now that you've written out five happy memories from your past and associated them with the feelings that these memories brought you, think about the most recent happy memory you've had. Close your eyes and allow the memory and the emotions that accompany it to flood your body.

EXERCISE
Creating Your Emotional Blueprint

Once you've learned to connect with the feelings that sing to your individual soul, you're going to create a blueprint that will be as unique as your fingerprint.

1. Write out the five memories from the previous exercise in chronological order.

2. For each memory, ask yourself, What was I feeling during the exact moment of the memory? Write down everything that comes to mind.

3. Once you've written out all the memories and the emotions they evoked, make a separate list of the emotions in no particular order. For example, for my memory of spending time with my mom at the beach, the associated emotions were excitement and connection.

4. Identify your top emotions from all five events. You may have some repeated emotions (and that's okay), but just write them once.

    The list of emotions from my five events included

    1. Connection
    2. Excitement
    3. Passion
    4. Joy
    5. Love
    6. Empathy

EXERCISE
Discovering Your Primary and Secondary Emotions

Human psychology studies have shown over the years that we're all driven by one primary emotion in conjunction with an underlying secondary emotion. It's now time to determine yours.

1. Once you have your list of emotions written out, compare the first emotion on your list with the second and ask yourself which you'd rather feel.

2. Take the answer to that and compare it to the third emotion.

3. Work your way down the list in this fashion. We will use my list in the previous section as an example.

    *   Would you rather feel connected or excited? My answer is connected.

    *   Would you rather feel connected or passionate? My answer is connected.

    *   Would you rather feel connected or joyful? My answer is connected.

    *   Would you rather feel connected or love? My answer is connected.

    *   Would you rather feel connected or empathy? My answer is connected.

    This exercise shows me that my primary emotion is feeling connected.

4. Once you've completed this exercise for your primary emotion, repeat the same exercise, except leave your identified primary emotion off the list.

Of course, your primary emotion will likely be different than mine. When I completed this exercise, my secondary emotional driver was excitement. When I completed this list with my best friend, her primary emotion was her need to feel love. Her secondary emotional driver was the need to feel connected. She had lost both of her parents when she was twelve, and those two emotions were driving forces in her life because of these earlier life experiences.

Once you've gone through this exercise, you'll understand the top two emotions that personally drive you. This will enable you to create what we call your *emotional blueprint statement*. As you move through life, your primary and secondary emotions may change. But let's focus on what they are right now and find a way to work with them.

EXERCISE
Creating Your Emotional Blueprint Statement

It's time to create your own emotional blueprint statement. Take the top two emotions that drive you from the previous exercise and, in your journal, write out a concise statement as follows.

My emotional blueprint statement is as follows:

> *I, Melissa B, have two primary emotions that drive me. My primary emotion is the need to feel connected. My secondary emotion is the desire to feel excitement from helping others.*

When I read the sentence, I know it's exactly what my personal truth is. Now it's your turn.

> *I, _____, have two primary emotions that drive me. My primary emotion is _____. My secondary emotion is my desire to feel_____.*

Once you've done this, read the sentence out loud and see if it resonates with your soul.

Understanding the Strengths, Talents, and Skills That Make You Unique

Now that you've identified your primary and secondary emotions and which feelings you want to associate with your life purpose, let's dig deeper and determine what your strengths, talents, and skills are. It's usually the things that we are naturally good at that assist in determining what our life's purpose should be.

Some of you might already have an idea of what your strengths, talents, and skills are. If you aren't so lucky, the following exercises will help you to uncover them.

EXERCISE
Uncovering Your Strengths, Talents, and Skills

1. **Create a "Love List."** Write down all of the activities that you love to do in life. Be outrageous, open-minded, honest, and creative. The point is to get inspired and let your imagination run free.

2. **List the things you do with relative ease.** The very activities you're passionate about may end up being your purpose, but because they're so natural and under your nose, you may not be aware of them.

3. **Look back at your personal history to see what you have overcome.** Everyone has unique challenges that they've had to overcome. This gives you a perspective that no one else has. What have you conquered and need to share to make the world a better place? Life events are additional clues and the universe's way of pointing you toward your life purpose. We'll have a chance to dig deeper into life events later in this chapter.

4. **Ask trusted friends, family, and professional coaches for their perspective.** If you're stuck figuring out what lights your fire and can't shake off

your own inner critic, it may be time for objectivity. Other people will see things that you don't and can help guide you to something hidden inside of yourself. What do other people say you're really good at, or should do professionally, or do more of? When you write these suggestions down, do you feel the top two emotions we identified earlier? If not, don't fall into the trap of allowing others to influence you into choosing a direction that doesn't resonate with your soul.

5. **Answer these thought-provoking self-discovery questions:**

    - What are the things you would do even if you didn't get paid for them?

    - What are two personal qualities that you know you possess? Consider some examples: inspiring, enthusiastic, artistic, humorous, courageous, creative, athletic, ambitious, driven, committed, resilient, reliable, patient, passionate, optimistic, great networker-connector, self-confident.

    - What are two worldly causes that are important to you or two ways in which you want to impact the world?

    - What is the one thing you want to experience or accomplish before you die?

    - If you had all the money in the world, how would you spend your time?

    - What would your perfect day look like? Describe every detail.

    - What activities set your soul on fire?

Once you've answered these questions, you should have a good idea of what your strengths and talents are. It is helpful to further consolidate your list into your top strengths and talents. For example, my top list consisted of

- Networking and connecting
- Helping others
- Public speaking
- Listening

- Writing
- Creating
- Sales and marketing
- Empathy
- Leading
- Mentoring, coaching, and encouraging others
- Finances and working with numbers

Once you've compiled your list, complete the following exercise to identify your own strengths and talents to assist you in determining your life purpose.

You may have an idea of what you'd like to do with your life. If this is the case, it's great to start thinking with the end in mind. For example, if you are a skilled debater and want to become a lawyer, learn about the different kinds of attorneys, the classes you'll have to take to become a lawyer, and so on.

All of this planning can start as young as high school. It might start later, should you decide to become a lawyer at a different point in your life. Start reading books that specialize in your purpose. It is ideal to start as young as possible once you've identified your purpose.

Before jumping into this next exercise, let's hear how Anastasia was able to take her strengths and talents of problem solving and deep empathy for others and turn it into a thriving profession of what she calls a true "education disrupter."

CLUE

"But the Hebrew word, the word
timshel—'Thou mayest'—that gives a
choice. It might be the most important
word in the world. That says the way
is open. That throws it right back
on a man. For if 'Thou mayest'—it is
also true that 'Thou mayest not.'"

**—FROM *EAST OF EDEN* BY
JOHN STEINBECK**

Anastasia Hall
EDUCATION DISRUPTOR

My name is Anastasia Hall, and I am an education disruptor. I could refer to myself as a teacher and even an entrepreneur, given where my career has gone in these past few years, but I choose education disruptor because that's my purpose.

People enter the education field for different reasons: some because they were inspired by a teacher, some because they don't know what other path to follow, and some because they want to fix the institution they spent so many years frustrated by. I fall into the third category.

Ultimately, I am a deeply empathetic problem-solver. I see adults through the context of their upbringing and access (or lack of access) to opportunities. I see educational institutions as severely lacking in both innovation and people with entrepreneurial mindsets ready to identify the causes of problems and execute on long-term solutions.

Think of the number of formative years we spend in educational institutions and juxtapose it with how many people feel void of any purpose or path. I found my purpose in my lackluster experiences as a student and my continued frustration as a classroom teacher.

But now I wake up every morning with the intention of creating dynamic spaces where kids can learn who they are, and develop what they can do, so they can walk into the world as adults who confidently claim value within it.

I was born in Brooklyn, New York, to an incredibly generous father and an equally kind mother. The level of shyness that consumed me as a kid was in some ways crippling, except I was confident in my academic and emotional intelligence at school. I was afraid to ask a server at a restaurant for ketchup, but I was not afraid to raise my hand in class or help a peer with their homework.

I attended one of the top specialized public high schools in Manhattan. I was at the top of my class and knew I wanted to spend my life in education but lacked any connection to my teachers or administrators. For college, I knew I wanted to be a teacher, but based on my experiences in high school, I did not want those same people to guide me on how to teach, so I majored in history, which was most relevant to me because it was the study of the choices people make and the outcomes of those choices.

I attended New York University (NYU) for undergrad, and Teachers College, Columbia University for grad school. Both are very prestigious and very expensive schools. I emerged from both with an incredible amount of experience, but also debt-free, thanks to my dad. In my mind, I was the type of person who should go into teaching. Imagine coming from those two universities with huge debt and walking into a profession that starts at $48,000—not a realistic possibility. But for me and my position, it was absolutely a choice I wanted to make and had the privilege of making.

I loved NYU. The professors were incredibly engaged, and it afforded me my first teaching opportunities. Not all public schools receive health education, so a group of us were trained to deliver a multipiece health education curriculum. We would travel throughout the city to various schools, where I taught high school students (only a few years removed from me) about sexually transmitted infections and abusive relationships.

I graduated NYU cum laude, took my three-month summer vacation to live with family friends in Greece, and then went directly into graduate school at Teachers College, Columbia University.

Columbia was the top education program at the time, and one of the reasons was their unique teaching master's degree structure. Normally, a teaching master's degree entails two years: the first is spent in graduate classes learning about pedagogy (the art and science of teaching) and building fake lesson plans. The second is spent student teaching in real high schools.

The traditional structure keeps you so far away from the reality of teaching that despite all your time studying new and progressive pedagogy, once you get to the classroom a year later, you revert to your almost two decades of experience as a student in the classroom and just follow the actions of the teachers you weren't necessarily all that inspired by.

Columbia puts both years into one full calendar year. We taught during the day and went to our graduate classes at night. We could apply the pedagogy in real time. It was brutal but the most effective way to train. We were starting to understand and assess the quality of our ability to deliver on it.

For my first stint, I taught in East Harlem. For my second, Chelsea. They were both public schools and yet a world away from each other in terms of resources. In my mind, I was going to work myself all the way to superintendent of NYC public schools to enact equity in our educational institutions.

The year I graduated from Columbia, New York City had a teacher hiring freeze. The school in Chelsea offered me a job, but I couldn't take it, so I worked per diem for a year to see if I could wait out the freeze. The freeze won. So I applied to every private school in the city and received an interview with only one school—but one was all I needed. I had a horrible first year of teaching, like we all do. I made every mistake I could possibly make, but I kept pushing my curriculum to be truly student-centered. Ninety percent of the criteria I used to evaluate my performance and impact as a teacher was relevance. By the time I finished my five years of teaching at the school, I knew two things: students didn't need to be tested and they didn't need homework.

Although private school teachers have more autonomy—and in some cases better benefits—we don't make enough money to live in a place like New York City. So I left New York City for Florida. I found a private school that fit my ethos, met my future husband at my interview due to a scheduling mistake (another story for another time), and came to push forward thinking around curriculum design.

I found myself teaching the classes that no history or social studies teacher wants to teach: economics and business. But I loved them, because they were deeply, inherently relevant to students. As the popularity of these classes—and the financial literacy class I wrote—continued to rise, my head of school sent me to our sister school to check out an entrepreneurship program, The Startup Studio, that was recommended to them. I drove three hours up to Orlando, and at around 8:30 a.m. my career took a pivot that I couldn't have foreseen: I met my business partner, Gary Conroy.

Gary was a serial entrepreneur and founder and CEO of The Startup Studio, a brand-new type of entrepreneurial program—one that ignored all academic measures and only cared for marketplace credibility. This program creates a forum for students to take their business ideas to various entrepreneurs who provide feedback that enables them to propel their dreams into a reality. He was in his third year of being a classroom facilitator for the program.

After the visit, we began working together to bring the program to my school successfully. Then I joined his team as the director of education and was valued enough to earn equity in the company. We expanded further into the private sphere, and this year, the program entered the public school system, coming full circle for me.

Here's what I've learned thirteen years into my teaching career and three years into my entrepreneurial journey: to disrupt the system, you have to get inside of it while maintaining the integrity of your core values. Individuals and institutions don't love change, but once you've established measurable impact, you can put change in your mission statement.

EXERCISE

Connect Your Top Five Strengths, Talents, and Skills to Your Emotional Blueprint Statement

It's time to examine your strengths, talents, and skills from the last exercise and see if they align with your emotional blueprint statement that you created earlier.

1. Create your list of strengths, talents, and skills into descending order, starting with your greatest strength. Try to narrow your list down further to the top five strengths, talents, and or skills that you possess. For example, my top five strengths noted above are networking, helping others, writing, empathy, and sales and marketing.

2. Once you have your list of strengths, talents, and skills, write your emotional blueprint statement next to each one of them. It may seem repetitive, but go with it.

3. If you're having trouble narrowing your list down to your top five, review your list and answer the following questions:

    -   When you are engaging in these activities or utilizing these strengths, how does it make you feel?

- Does each strength/talent and/or skill bring out the primary and secondary emotions that make your soul sing?

4. Ensure that each of those strengths identified resonates with your soul. If they don't, cross them off the list.

Really concentrate on all the emotions and feelings in your body throughout these activities. For example, my top strength is networking. As I sit back and picture myself networking, I get a rush of adrenaline that fills my entire body. I find myself filled with excitement and get a feeling of connection with others. Going back to my own primary and secondary emotions—my strong ability to *connect* with others leading to enriched lives and my personal *excitement from helping others*—I know that I'm on the right path.

In this chapter, you've identified your top two emotions, you understand your top strengths, talents, and skills, and have identified a cause-and-effect relationship between the two.

Let's take a moment and combine your strengths, talents, and skills with your driving emotions to create your life purpose statement.

EXERCISE
Creating Your Life Purpose Statement

Take a moment and write out your emotional blueprint statement from the earlier exercise.

For example, my emotional blueprint statement is as follows:

> *I, Melissa B, have two primary emotions*
> *that drive me. My primary emotion is to feel*
> *connected. My secondary emotion is the desire to*
> *feel excitement from helping others.*

Take a moment and further narrow down your top five strengths and talents from five to two.

For example, my top two strengths and talents are networking and helping others.

Take a moment and combine the two in order to come up with your own life purpose statement.

For example, my life purpose statement would read as follows:

> *I, Melissa B, was born with the strengths and talents of <u>networking</u> and <u>helping others.</u> When I am networking and helping others I feel a sense of <u>connection</u> to others, which makes me feel <u>excited.</u>*

When I read the sentence, I know it's exactly what my personal truth is.

Now, it's your turn to combine your emotional blueprint statement with your top two strengths and talents to come up with your life purpose statement.

> *I, _____, was born with the strengths and talents of _____ and _____. When I am _____ 'and _____, I feel a sense of _____ and _____.*

Once you have identified your emotional blueprint and life purpose statements, you have the initial blueprint to further define what your ultimate purpose should look like. You might not know the exact industry, job title, position, or career path you wish to take, but you're much closer to understanding what makes you happy. Don't worry so much about putting an exact definition or title on things. That will come. Once you begin to identify the clues in your life, your exact purpose will become clear.

For example, I knew that I wanted to pursue something that would allow me to network and help people. I had no idea that it would be somewhere in the medical field until I started acknowledging all of the events and people (clues) in my life that led me into choosing the medical field.

One of my earliest life events (clues) was when my arm was severed at age nine. There would be many more clues in my life that pointed my purpose toward the medical field. At the time, I wasn't tuned into recognizing the clues and would have to encounter many more medical challenges in order to fully recognize my ultimate purpose in life. A huge clue for everyone should be when something continues repeating itself over and over again in the form of different events and experiences. Once there are recurring themes surrounding our lives, it's a part of a bigger sign that you may need to recognize.

In this next chapter, we'll look at the events that have occurred in your life up to this moment. It's the clues within these life events that will ultimately lead you to your life purpose. It's your job to become more aware of how and why these events and people have shown up in your life. It isn't the event or person itself that holds the key; it's what we learn and choose to do with the event that shapes our ultimate destiny.

Clues can come to you in the form of an inner feeling or hunch. Once we have identified each one of these clues for our own lives, we can begin to connect the dots and create our own treasure map, enabling our inner compass to lead us that much closer to our personal treasure.

You hold the key within that allows you to become a clue catcher and, eventually, a clue connector. What if, instead of looking back and connecting the dots, we suddenly had the ability to see the dots as we proceed forward? That is our goal together, and MY goal for YOU.

> ### T R E A S U R E   H U N T   R U L E
> *Be sure to pay attention*
> *to your inner feelings,*
> *hunches, and intuition.*

Follow the Clues

- Understand the difference between your purpose, goals, and vision. It starts with your vision, which can be further defined by your life purpose, which can be further broken down into SMART goals.

- Identify your primary and secondary emotions by completing the ten-minute exercise mentioned in this chapter.

- Once you've identified the primary and secondary emotions that resonate with you, complete the exercise in this chapter to come up with your own emotional blueprint statement.

- Identify the strengths, talents, and skills that are unique to you by completing the exercise in this chapter.

- Once you've identified your top five strengths, talents, and skills, see if they're aligned with your emotional blueprint statement. If they aren't, cross them off your list. If they are, you're one step closer to identifying your life purpose.

- Take the time to combine your emotional blueprint statement with your top two strengths, talents, and skills to formulate your own personal life purpose statement.

- Don't worry about coming up with an exact title, position, industry, or career path. Focus on the awareness of what you are great at and what drives you emotionally. The rest will come in time and with your ability to recognize the clues in your own life.

9

BECOMING A CLUE CATCHER AND CONNECTOR

Step 8: Identifying Clues through Events, People, Places, and Life Experiences

If I told you that all life events, both good and bad, ultimately lead each of us to our God-given purpose, would you embrace life a little differently? Another way to say it is that everything in life happens for a reason. That's right, everything is happening to you because it turns you into the person you're becoming.

I'm sure some of you agree and others will likely be angry. You may be thinking, how could something so bad be predetermined? And why me? Good or bad, everything that has happened to you has shaped your life. Every life event and person you meet along your journey has been placed in your life for a purpose. It's your job to recognize this and seize the opportunities as they arise. These events and people should be looked at as additional clues that assist in the creation of your own personal road map, leading you that much closer to your own treasures.

It's time to start thinking about the events, big and small, that have gotten you to where you are today. We've focused on the powers of our mind in many of the previous chapters. That will help you in creating a sustainable and insurmountable foundation. It will help you overcome challenges in life and view life differently. We have a better understanding of what our own personal strengths, talents, and skills are, and what drives us emotionally.

It's time to shift our focus to the events, people, and experiences that have touched our hearts and brought out emotions and feelings that we wish to harness and repeat. Events in our lives shape our thinking, beliefs, and overall attitude. When I ask people about the things that have shaped their lives, they come up with big stuff, mainly traumatic events that were hard to ignore, but smaller events shape us too.

Small Things Do Matter

If you want to truly understand your life purpose, take a look at the events in your life that made you feel like you were alive. Ask yourself, What memories set my soul on fire? I have personally found that it wasn't the significant events—like getting a major award or a big payday—that mattered the most. It was spending quality time walking on the beach with my mom, helping my clients achieve their goals, and experiencing fun times with the women I've been mentoring.

It's often the small events that add up to create the big things. Once you start to think about the events that have had a big impact on your life, and how those events made you feel, you're a few steps closer to understanding your life purpose.

Once you realize that all of the things happening are essentially building blocks to help you reach your highest self, it becomes easier to deal with all the pain, setbacks, and struggles that you've had to encounter to get where you're headed.

Recognizing the Aha Moments

Have you ever experienced that "aha" moment when everything finally made sense? It's a moment when all the confusion you once had finally dissipates. You sit back and realize just how strong you are, and why things unfolded the way that they did. This is not to say that life doesn't throw us some curveballs, which can make anyone question their sanity from time to time. When we can say that life doesn't happen *to* us, it happens *for* us, we acknowledge through a conscious choice that we are willing to perceive challenges as something beneficial. This allows us to handle life's challenges in the most productive and joyful way.

I want you to take a moment to repeat the previous sentence to yourself: Life doesn't happen *to* us, it happens *for* us.

Say it out loud, and let it resonate with you. Setbacks are Setups to teach us great lessons and to take us closer to our life purpose. We can't control some of the events that have happened to us, but we can control our reactions to them. This statement is so important and worth repeating. We can't control all life events, but we have complete control of how we react to them. Look at these events as clues for your personal road map.

This next section and the following exercises are designed to help further uncover your life purpose. We understand the emotions that drive us and what our unique qualities, strengths, and talents are. We are starting to realize what core values are important in our lives. We're now ready to figure out how we can turn this into our life purpose. Earlier, I was able to identify my top emotions as excitement and feeling connected to others. I came up with my top strengths and talents list, which includes networking, creating, writing, sales and marketing, and helping others.

So now what? How can I use this knowledge about myself to come up with a profession that would allow me to monetize this into my life purpose and profession? How can you?

My life events guided me toward helping others in the medical field because of what I had personally gone through as a patient. You've already learned about my severed right arm. In addition, I was involved in several automobile accidents early in life, which left me with broken bones. At sixteen, I was diagnosed with abnormal dysplasia of the cervix leading to precancerous cells. I had to undergo cryosurgery, which was a painful procedure. You have already learned about the anxiety I experienced during college.

TREASURE HUNT RULE
*Each clue leads to another,
eventually leading to your treasure.*

The events that seemed scary earlier in my life ended up being the reason I chose a profession in the medical field. These events were merely clues that assisted in the creation of my personal road map, which led to my treasures in life. I took these experiences and managed to find the good lessons that these events taught me. They certainly impacted me, and I chose to let the impact become my internal compass for the future direction of my life instead of becoming a victim. I did not want patients to experience the same kind of fear that I once had as a patient.

Growing up, I took the time to journal about all of these life situations. This allowed me to dig deep within and to determine the true meaning behind these experiences. I was essentially creating a journal of the major life events, their deeper meaning, and the positive outcomes that I would take with me throughout my life.

It's time to start thinking about the events, big and small, that have gotten you to where you are today. It's time to create your own aha moments and understand why some of the events that you have personally encountered have occurred.

We have focused on the power of our mind in many of the previous chapters. It's time to shift our focus to the events, people, and experiences that touched our hearts and brought out emotions and feelings that we wish to harness and repeat. Events in our life shape our thinking, beliefs, and overall attitude. When I ask others about the events and people that have shaped their life, they come up with big things, mainly traumatic events that were hard to ignore.

I can relate to this, because when I worked on my own list, the first memories that came up were the big ones—medical issues and procedures as early as middle school, being fired from a dream job, divorce, losing a lawsuit, and other painful failures. I did have some positive, wonderful, exciting events too:

- The double wedding ceremony with my mom back in 2000
- Graduating from college
- Many fun trips that I have experienced with my dad and stepmother
- Attending my niece and nephew's graduation
- The birth of my niece and nephew
- Building a successful M&A firm with my stepfather
- Working with my lifelong mentor
- Becoming a self-made millionaire twice in one lifetime

Focusing on the big events is natural. However, I believe that the small things, the ones that we neglect to pay attention to, contribute to how we conduct ourselves in a way that we hardly recognize. Often, when we talk to our friends, they bring up their past and examine it; they talk about small incidents that were big for them at the time, even out of proportion.

A friend once told me about the most embarrassing moment of her life. For years, she couldn't give presentations in public because when she was eleven she stood in front of her classmates and her voice sounded squeaky, like a boy going through puberty.

Although we may be unaware of these little events, they can have a great influence over the trajectory of our lives. Think about it as if you were on a treasure hunt. Every clue in your path (event in your life) affects you in one of three ways:

1. Has no impact, so you just keep going,

2. Becomes a part of who you are and increases your likelihood of finding the treasure (energy, motivation), so you keep going in the same direction, but smaller obstacles no longer matter, or

3. Changes your direction.

If you understand that every event in life falls under one of these categories, you will agree that we tend to ignore the ones that have no impact on our direction and take notice of the other two—the ones that give us a boost and the ones that change our direction.

Happy and Unhappy Events

It's tempting to think that we get a boost of serotonin from happy events and our direction changes due to unhappy ones, but this isn't necessarily true. Sometimes unhappy events help us move forward faster and take bolder actions.

A perfect example of an unhappy event that motivates people is getting really sick. This causes many people to take charge of their lives and finally do all the activities they've only dreamed of before. I suspect that the COVID-19 virus is having this effect on many people. Even if we don't personally get the virus, the very thought of it has made many people make major life changes.

An example of a happy event that triggers a huge change is going away to college for the first time. I remember how my life changed drastically. I moved over 800 miles away from home for the first time in my life and was thrown into an environment that included brand-new friends and surroundings.

As you reflect on your own life, take out your journal and complete the following exercise.

> **TREASURE HUNT RULE**
> *Most clues are subjective,*
> *so everyone's list of events*
> *will be personalized.*

EXERCISE

50 Life Events (That Have Already Happened)

This exercise is simple: write out a list of fifty life events that have changed and shaped your life up to this moment. This also includes people you've met along the way. Keep in mind the three ways that every clue in your path can affect you.

TIPS TO HELP YOU WRITE OUT YOUR LIST

If you have trouble coming up with fifty events or people, here are some helpful tips:

- Stick to meaningful events, and don't write obvious ones like "I was born."

- Write events that have changed your life from *your* perspective, not someone else's. So don't include someone else's memories—for example, "My mom said this event changed me."

- If you have experienced several events with common themes, this is likely a clue. Take some time to meditate and go within as you assess these events and write out the underlying message. As you begin to get centered with yourself, your intuition will guide you in the right direction.

- Going over events in chronological order may help you uncover more details about your life. Go over memories from childhood, as early as three years of age. If you remember them, they were probably meaningful.

- Think of special birthdays that have shaped your life or a gift you remember specifically.

- Think of family gatherings (holidays, birthdays, anniversaries, summer vacations). Family gatherings can be awesome and change your life.

- The birth of a sibling seems to be a popular event that many people feel has changed their life.

- Find meaningful times at school, from first grade to higher education: exams, awards, school breaks, parties, report cards, challenges, failures, horrible teachers, angel teachers who have helped you become who you are today.

- Consider times when you changed schools or moved homes; trips taken with family, friends, or another group; and places that you've visited.

- Recall something good someone has done for you—a good word, an expression of trust, a loving statement, help, support, an act of kindness that you appreciate and store in your memory and that has changed the way you think or feel.

- Think about something unpleasant someone has done to you (from your perspective) or a fight you've had with someone. Conflicts, fights, and arguments can be boosters or changers.

- Write down the books you've read that have changed your life. I don't know about you, but I've read books that have changed me forever. When I go to the bookstore, the books that I need at that moment tend to present themselves.

- Consider successes and victories that have changed your life. Many times, successes are great boosters and help us build motivation to move toward our desired destination. Consider the failures that have changed your life.

- First job, best job, volunteer activities that exposed you to new challenges.

- Can you think of any unexpected events or surprises that changed your life?

- Include people you've met who have changed your path and shaped your life. When I think of my own list, it includes several people who've made a difference in my life, and I carry some part of them with me.

- Recall friends you've had over the years and what you learned from each of them. Try to think of two or three friends from each level of your education. Friends play a huge role in the shaping of our lives. I believe that friends we've had over the years are there to teach us the best lessons of our lives. If you come up with a list of twenty good friends from various times of your life and think of what each of them has given you and under what circumstances, your list will be on track.

CLUE

"Trust your own instincts; go inside and follow your heart right from the start. Stand up for what you believe in. As I have learned, that's the path to happiness."

—LESLEY ANN WARREN

After you've written your list, review each item and think about the following questions:

- Did this event boost you up or change your direction, and how?
- Can you identify a connection between your top five strengths or talents and this event?
- Could this event be a hidden clue toward what your life purpose might be?
- As you look back at your top fifty events, do you see any common or recurring themes that could be clues leading you toward your purpose? Once you can identify these themes and the lessons that you derive from these events, be sure to follow your heart.
- Are there any conclusions that you can make about how these events have shaped you into the person that you are?
- Can you identify a connection between this event and your primary and secondary emotions? In what ways?

You may recall that one of my life events was spending a summer doing community service for something that I had gotten into trouble for earlier that year. I worked that summer at a local blood bank. Through this experience, I felt a real sense of excitement and connection in helping others.

This was one of my life events that brought out my primary and secondary emotions and allowed me to experience networking, helping others, and being exposed to marketing. These happen to be three of my top five strengths. Ironically, an event that started out as a punishment for something I had done wrong ended up being an aha moment and leading me toward a career in the laboratory diagnostic profession.

At the time, I wasn't able to put the pieces of the puzzle together and fully comprehend the cause-and-effect relationship between the events, but today, some thirty-three years later, it all makes perfect sense.

The key with this exercise is to start recognizing patterns that emerge within your own life and start connecting the reasons for some of these events. Try to apply a positive mindset to events that may have been negative at the time. For example, I had several negative medical situations occur when I was younger. However, looking back, I recognize that these were my clues that motivated me to choose a profession in the medical field. I wanted patients to have a better experience then I had experienced. What situations have occurred in your life that you viewed as negative? Was this event placed in your life to point you in a direction to reach your ultimate life purpose?

EXERCISE
50 Life Events (That You Want to Achieve)

In addition to listing out fifty life events, write out another fifty activities that you would like to accomplish in your life. This list can include anything from running your first 5K or getting a specific degree to jumping out of an airplane while skydiving! It can also include people you would like to meet, hobbies you want to become involved in, and places you want to travel to.

Leading with Your Heart

You've identified the emotions that make your soul sing, figured out your strengths and talents, identified both small and large life events, and brought all these components together as you carefully reviewed your fifty top life events. Some of you have already determined exactly what your life purpose is, while others may be scratching their heads. Either way, that's okay. You're exactly where you're supposed to be, and it's time to get out of your head and lead with your heart.

Your compass and guiding light from this point forward is your heart. It's your inner voice, or divine power, that will lead you to your ultimate life purpose. When you follow your heart—putting your God first, followed by yourself and then others—you will uncover your purpose in life. Remember, you must put your God first, then yourself, then others. This is healthy and will ensure that you maintain your personal power. Your heart always knows the truth and will know what the next steps are. If you've been living in your head, get out of your own way.

When we lead with our heart, we cease to have regrets. We start learning how to trust our instincts. This becomes easier when we practice daily meditations. Our heart will ultimately guide us in the right direction. We gain a newfound respect for ourself and those around us. We begin to focus on what truly matters instead of what we think should matter.

Following our heart ensures that we get to know who we really are and what matters to us. It's amazing what happens when we get out of our own way. We might surprise ourselves. Leading with the heart ensures that we're on the right path. If we have a sense of unease or ambiguity about something, we know that we're on the wrong path. Our heart always guides us toward our true direction and calling in life.

Following our heart allows us to let go of grudges, past hurts, and stuff that doesn't matter in the end. Once we let go of this negative energy, we are forgiving ourselves and focusing on the present. This is when miracles start to happen.

Learning to love ourselves first will allow us to love others. Once we recognize that all of the bad experiences that have happened in our lives have made us the wonderful, strong person that we are today, we'll be able to love ourselves and show kindness to everyone we meet.

Trusting our intuition allows us to lead with our heart. Once we have mastered this, life will flow naturally. It's important to stop overthinking and learn to go with what life throws at us. Once we truly believe that everything happens for a reason, we start to look at life events and the people that we meet differently. We show up to life with a newfound level of confidence. We start to recognize the clues and life becomes an adventure.

In conclusion, listen to your heart—it's the only way to know your true desires and what genuinely makes you feel fulfilled. Once we learn to get honest with ourselves, the possibilities become endless. Our life purpose and legacy will open up, and before we know it, we will be living our dream life.

Let's take a moment and hear how Zola led with her heart, followed her intuition to move across the country to chase her dreams. She had developed a skill as a teenager of sewing, and would turn it into a lifelong passion by becoming a fashion icon for many well-known stars and celebrities. She even met her husband while pursuing her love for fashion.

Zola Keller

ENTREPRENEUR, FASHION DESIGNER

"Never accept no and never say no if you want to be a successful entrepreneur."

ONE CHAPTER ENDS, AND A NEW ONE BEGINS

It was the winter of 1971, and I was twenty-four years old. It had been a brutally cold, windy season even for my hometown of Chicago.

I had always liked working. When I was fourteen, I landed my first job as a telemarketer. I don't remember what I was selling, but they gave me a script, and if I got through it without the person hanging up, I had done well. Later, in high school, I worked as a cashier at a bowling alley on Chicago's South Side.

But on this winter day, work wasn't providing its typical enjoyment, and everything was dark, inside and out. By then, I was at the Big Ben Chemical order house downtown working as a PBX telephone operator. I knew this was not what I wanted to do with the rest of my life.

My father had just died. I was recently divorced and had a two-year-old girl at home. There was a terrible snowstorm blowing outside. The weather was so bad that the roads became impassable, forcing me to trudge home through wet knee-high snow.

Involuntarily, my mind traveled to South Florida, where my parents had a vacation home. When I had visited in the past, I would play tennis all day in the warm sun, building up a sweat to perfect my forehand and backhand in pursuit of mastering my favorite hobby.

Fond memories and my current miserable, bone-chilling situation combined to decide for me: with my father gone and my mother grieving, it was time to close the chapter on my childhood in Chicago. I would start a new one where there was no such thing as a snowstorm, where you could play tennis from sunrise to sunset.

I packed up my little girl, Terri, my mother, Bernice, and everything I could fit into our 1970 Buick Riviera. I sat in the passenger seat as my mother drove us the 1,400 miles through Nashville and then Atlanta on the way to Fort Lauderdale. It was the first time I had seen mountains, and I was petrified. Terri stood on the back seat and covered my eyes as we wound our way down toward sea level.

When we finally arrived, we set ourselves up in a little apartment on the beach in Lauderdale-by-the-Sea. I needed to find a job, but I was set on one that would provide me the freedom to pursue tennis in the afternoons. I picked up a sales position in a high-end women's clothing store, but I was hungry to create my own business. I knew I'd never be happy being someone else's employee.

A CROCHET HOOK AND A PRAYER

My aunt had taught me how to crochet and knit when I was a teenager. I never thought I'd use that skill. It was now

1972 and crocheting and knitting were all the rage among older women. I was also living on the beach, so I constantly saw young and not-so-young women wearing bikinis. Next to them, inevitably, were older women sitting under the Florida sun knitting and crocheting for their children and grandchildren. Then it struck me: why not crochet bikinis? They were just two connected triangles for the top half and a patch for the bottom half. How hard could it be?

I started churning out my first bikinis and selling the merchandise at the beach shops, walking into one after the other from Miami to Palm Beach. People began placing orders. Then the shop owners started asking for other things like cover-ups, shawls, and sweaters. I was shocked—I hadn't expected this to catch on. I enlisted some of those older women who were crocheting as a hobby, offering to pay them to turn out my designs.

My business was growing, and I didn't know what I was doing. I did know that I was taking orders and making some money. Someone told me to get advice at SCORE, a nonprofit of retired businesspeople, lawyers, and accountants who teach people how to be entrepreneurs. It was hard for me, but I wanted to show these accomplished men what I was doing. What would they think of my little endeavor? I showed them my order book and asked them what to do next. They said the first thing to do was start buying yarn at wholesale instead of retail, as I had been doing up to that point.

A BUSINESS CONNECTION THAT TURNS INTO SOMETHING MORE

In Fort Lauderdale, there was only one place I knew that sold yarn; it was a storefront called Yarns Galore. I went in and told the gentleman standing behind the counter what I was doing and that I needed a lot of yarn at wholesale. He said it was a great idea, and I brought him to my car to show him a trunk filled with just-crocheted merchandise. He saw my enthusiasm and energy. It turned out that he was Yarns Galore's owner and formally trained in the fashion industry.

He offered to do me one better than providing whole-sale yarn. If we'd become partners, he said, he'd help get the business going and supply the raw materials. I could focus on design—and not just bikinis but knit suits and dresses. I said yes on the spot. My new partner's name was Ave, and it turned out he would eventually become my husband. This was simply a clue that I was on the right path. I was following my passion, and subsequently met my life partner. Years later, he would say that he based his offer on recognizing a young woman with drive, an extraordinary sense of style, and a ton of chutzpah.

We started building the business and more orders came in. I got an appointment with the South Florida buyer for Saks Fifth Avenue, my biggest potential customer up to that point. She said she'd try my designs out at one local store to see how they did. Within days of hitting the sales floor, customers had purchased all the pieces we'd provided. We were a huge success! They decided to put my designs into five stores across the country.

Katharine Ross, the original star of *The Stepford Wives*, purchased one of my knit dresses from the Saks store in Palo Alto, California. She wore it for an artist who sketched her as the prototype of robotic women. I was never told of the purchase because Saks took my label out and replaced it with theirs. I only learned of it when I saw my dress while watching the movie.

The Zola Keller name and reputation grew to the point where we opened a boutique on Oakland Park Boulevard. In 1982, we moved our headquarters to Las Olas Boulevard. Other locations would come and go: on Palm Beach's Worth Avenue, in the tony Bal Harbor Shops during the *Cocaine Cowboys* days, and across the peninsula in Bonita Springs. I was no longer the girl delivering yarn to two knitters and making $5 in profit on a $20 bikini.

My fashion scope grew with the desire to create, and my team and I are now internationally known for lavish gowns, with a clientele consisting of Miss Americas, entertainers, and stateswomen. We eventually provided gowns and costumes for Broadway shows and even cocktail outfits for The Boca Raton Beach Club. We created the garment for the reimagining of Miss Chiquita, the banana lady of the Chiquita Banana Company.

As my brand grew, my favorite and most joyous involvement by far came to be with brides and mothers. It is such an important day for them, and to be asked to be a small part of it is so rewarding. Brides come in with a detailed vision from childhood of what they want to wear. Sometimes it pushes our team to the limits of creativity, but we never say no.

Ave and I have had many adventures together along the way and some extraordinary highlights. I became the go-to fashion expert for the newspapers, magazines, and local TV stations—being called on by our local ABC television network affiliate to comment when Gianni Versace was killed in Miami, for example.

To give back to the community that has given us so much, we produced fashion shows to raise money for the causes in which we believe. Over time, we'd be involved in raising funds to end cystic fibrosis, feed senior citizens, provide care and comfort to animals in need, and give underprivileged children, survivors of domestic abuse, and those with cancer a helping hand.

All in all, like all business owners, I have seen both high times and challenging times. Our enterprises have gone from prospering to hurting and then back up again. All that just goes along with entrepreneurship. What allowed us to keep moving forward was my ongoing obsession with designing garments that make women look and feel beautiful. Looking back on the forty-seven years with Ave, our three kids, and the rest of the family and friends who have taken this adventure with us, I would not change a thing.

Follow the Clues

- Step 8 of finding your life purpose is to become your own clue catcher. This means that you have developed your own level of awareness and the deeper meaning of the people, places, and events that have occurred in your life. Dig deep and start becoming aware of the clues surrounding you. Once you have become aware, and started writing them down, you can later begin to connect the dots, becoming a clue connector.

- Write out the top fifty events, no matter the size, that have occurred in your life up to this moment. Be sure to remember that everything happens in your life for a reason and for your highest and greatest good. This may help provide a different perspective on the lessons that you draw from these events.

- Understand what you learned from these events and how they've shaped you into the person you are today. Take time to analyze your life events and whether they brought out your primary and secondary emotions.

- Look for the hidden clues in life events and the people that have crossed your path. Is the event or person trying to tell you something about your future?

- Learn to recognize and celebrate the aha moments along your journey.

- Learn to get out of your head and lead with your heart. When you lead with your heart, you will discover your life purpose.

10

LEARNING TO NAVIGATE

Step 9: Surrender Your Life Purpose to the Universe

Once you've determined your life purpose and created the road map toward your ultimate destiny, you'll need to surrender your desires to the universe to make them a reality. This doesn't mean that you don't work hard, set goals, and take action. It simply means that you relinquish control of the outcome. If you're like most people and try to control everything, you're probably asking these questions:

- How do I surrender?
- What do I need to do?
- How will I know once I have surrendered?

The natural tendency to control everything is ingrained in us, which makes it a challenge to surrender. Many people feel as if they are in this journey alone and need to make things happen. We feel as if we will lose all control if we take our hands off the wheel. We think we must navigate every twist and turn. However, learning to navigate is the complete opposite of this.

The entire point of surrendering is realizing that you have a magnificent force within you. You can call it spirituality, God, energy, or whatever you like. As you learned earlier with my story about fighting my legal battle for over a decade, it has taken me years and many battle scars to know what it feels like to truly surrender.

As humans we get stuck on the *doing* and all of the steps we think it *should* take to reach the end result. This is where anxiety takes over, and we become stressed, doubtful, and frustrated at times. We become so fixated on the plan or strategy and believe that it should be happening a specific way.

There are many benefits of surrendering to the universe:

- You begin to feel calm and connected to your purpose and path.

- You feel supported no matter what you're going through.

- You become aware of the blessings flowing through your life easily and effortlessly.

- You have a sense of peace and contentment in your life.

- You walk around with a sense of confidence and empowerment knowing that life events are flowing the way they are meant to, for the good of everyone and everything around you.

- You begin to recognize that not getting your way is simply God's way of redirecting you toward something much greater.

CLUE

"Surrender is like a fish finding the current and going with it."

—MARK NEPO

Why Do We Resist Surrendering?

In society, we've been taught that power equals control. The more control you have, the more power and success you have. This is a fallacy that we've been fed for generations. Furthermore, success, importance, and wealth do not equate to happiness.

For decades, humans have placed emphasis on having these ideals. But they are simply external achievements; whereas, your emotions are internal. You can create happiness, peace, and enjoyment now. So why the continued resistance to surrendering? It's merely overcoming the deep-rooted belief that having control of your life will provide you with everything you could possibly desire.

To many, control equals certainty. When you're in control, everything is certain. When you're certain, your level of control increases.

Each of us has control over only four items: our mindset, our choices, our actions, and our responses. When you understand this, you can begin to shift your perspective on trying to control the outcomes of everything in your life. You soon realize that letting go of control means you are finally in control.

Once you surrender to the universe, you begin carrying the belief that something better can happen. It's about knowing that you cannot see the bigger picture and trusting that the universe is always guiding you to your highest good. Surrendering allows you to receive blessings and opportunities you may have never noticed before. Surrendering allows you to flow with your soul's purpose. Surrendering puts you in control of how you're going to experience life, rather than how the end result will come to fruition.

Surrendering to the universe allows you to have enjoyable experiences right now, while the universe works behind the scenes to bring blessings and manifestations into your life.

In the next section, we'll review some of the tricks to make the process of surrendering to the universe much easier.

CLUE

"The moment of surrender is not when life is over. It's when it begins."

—MARIANNE WILLIAMSON

Be Happy Whether You've Accomplished Your Desire or Not

You'll know that you've been successful at surrendering when you're happy whether you've achieved your desire or not. It's living in a complete state of detachment from the outcome. You'll realize that your self-worth is not dependent on that desired outcome.

You'll have a sense of being complete, no matter what. You'll enjoying living in the present moment and will live your best life. You'll be grateful to have what you have and be where you are no matter what. You'll have no need for anything. There may be a strong desire and want for something, but you won't need it. When you let go of the neediness, you remove all resistance, and then whatever you desire can more easily flow into your life. It's how the energy of the universe works.

Have you ever noticed that when you like someone and want to date them, the more you present yourself as confident and happy with yourself, the more they become attracted to you? If you're needy and show too much interest, this doesn't allow the flow of energy, and that person won't have the space needed to become interested. Try it out sometime and watch the miracles that start to happen.

Feel Gratitude for the Present

As we learned in step 4 of our journey toward purpose, gratitude for what we have is key to attracting more. If you're looking at your current situation and don't feel good about it, you may end up losing some of the gifts that you currently have been blessed with. Learning to surrender and staying focused on everything that you have is another key to attracting more.

It's helpful to have a road map to work toward our life purpose, but be sure to allow for flexibility and detours along the journey. When things don't go exactly as planned, look for the things to be thankful for and focus on them.

Trust in Divine Timing

When we want something, we tend to want it *now*. We act like children and stomp our feet when things don't happen immediately. The reason that our wishes haven't manifested sooner is usually that we aren't ready to receive them. There may be a lesson that we or someone along the path must first learn before the thing we want manifests. We may need to do additional work. The bottom line is that we're simply not ready for it.

Have you heard the stories about people who won the lottery and ended up losing all of their money shortly thereafter? The main reason this happens is that the person didn't do the work to make sure their wealth was sustainable for the long term. When your desires don't happen overnight, be grateful for the time. It's a gift and clue that you have some additional work along your own journey. Once you've done the work, expanded your capacity to receive, and surrendered, your dreams will come together in *divine* timing, not yours.

Flex Your Faith Muscles

Having trust in the universe is like building your muscles. Strengthening takes a lot of practice. One way to do this is to create a list of different ways that the universe has come through in your life in a super magical way. For example, I was fired from a dream job only to be thrown into my ultimate destiny of becoming an entrepreneur and owning several companies.

At the time, being let go from a dream job was not what I wanted. My faith was tested, and I had a choice: to accept that God/the universe had a bigger and better purpose for my life, or to wallow in my own misery. Being fired was a huge clue in my life, preparing me for my real destiny. The people who were put in my path to fire me were perfectly aligned to further propel me toward my life purpose and all the victories that God had in store for me. They were merely some of my greatest clues.

I admit that I did sit in misery for quite a while after I was fired. I had to go through my own pity party, work through being a victim, until I woke up and recognized the opportunity that God put right in front of me. Every negative event can lead to a million positive ones. It's our choice, and the more we flex our faith muscles, the stronger they will become.

Surrendering Is a Daily Practice

Learning to surrender isn't something that comes overnight. It's a moment-by-moment decision. Whenever doubt, fear, and worry creep back into your mind, you have to be aware and recognize that you have a choice. You can simply say to yourself, I am choosing to surrender. It's that simple. It takes a willingness to give up the doubt and fear and let the rest go. The universe will help you do the rest.

It's your job to let the universe take the wheel. That means you hand things over. This doesn't mean that you don't prepare or fail to chart the course as we discussed earlier. It does mean giving up control of the outcome. You simply position yourself in the passenger seat and let the universe do its trick while you enjoy the ride. When you do this, you feel good. You know that events are happening behind the scenes for the good of all.

The trick is to stay alert, be aware, and surrender. The right people, places, and events will show up in your life to support your life purpose. Don't be surprised when they turn out even better than you ever dreamed. Dare to dream big and watch the magic.

EXERCISE

When Did You Let Go?

Take the next thirty minutes to write out some examples of when you let go of the need to control and surrendered, allowing your life to magically happen. It could have been a time when you really needed money, and it somehow randomly showed up. It could have been a time when you didn't get in to the college of your dreams, only to be accepted by your second-choice college, where you met the love of your life.

Follow the Clues

- Surrender your desires to the universe to make them a reality.

- Accept that you cannot see the bigger picture and trust that the universe is always guiding you to your highest good.

- When you let go of the need to be in control, you remove all resistance; whatever you desire can then more easily flow into your life.

11

THE KEY TO THE TREASURE CHEST

Step 10: Your Magical Future: Returning with the Elixir, and Giving Back

Melissa Butterworth
CEO, ENTREPRENEUR

CONNECTING MY OWN CLUES

1979, Waking Up after a Long Surgery

Did you wonder whatever happened to me after surgery to repair my arm? And why my father was in the hospital bed next to mine? I finally woke up in the recovery room after a four-hour surgery. My father was lying in the next bed. The sheets were tucked up all the way to his neck and his eyes were closed. He looked peaceful. My mom was sitting next to me, which brought me an immediate sense of peace.

Had my arm really been severed? Was this merely a bad dream? Why was my dad lying in the hospital bed next to me, with a band around his wrist and dressed in blue hospital scrubs? Or perhaps I had died and was getting a glimpse of heaven?

As I lay in the bed, half-conscious, I had no idea of the long road to recovery that lay in front of me. Just that morning, I had been playing with my friends on the playground, a fun-loving child with not a care in the world. In the blink of an eye, a fall off the seesaw, and my life would be forever changed, my destiny already predetermined. It would take me decades to uncover my own hidden treasure and ultimate life purpose. However, this event was certainly a guiding force and among the first of many clues for my life.

When I arrived at the hospital that day, unbeknownst to me, the doctors had pulled my parents aside to tell them that there was a 98 percent chance they would need to amputate my arm during surgery, as too much blood had been lost at the point of the breakage. I was going to need a prosthetic. I was right-handed, and it was my right arm that was damaged. Devastated, my dad fainted. He couldn't bear the thought of his only daughter growing up without an arm. He was admitted as an inpatient and put in the same hospital room, in the bed next to mine.

Unfortunately, the situation wasn't a dream. I never knew about that conversation until I became an adult. My parents had kept the prognosis with the doctors to themselves, and for that I am forever grateful. The thought that I'd likely lose my arm had never entered my subconscious, and no one had planted that seed in my mind.

Despite the less than 2 percent chance of saving my right arm, the doctors found a way to fix it, and I beat all odds. It took me eighteen months of physical therapy, hard work, dedication, resilience, and determination to relearn simple movements that we take for granted on a daily basis. I had to relearn how to eat, pick up my toothbrush, brush my hair, bathe, write, and do hundreds of other tasks. I eventually made it back to the tennis courts two years later. The intense scars from the surgery eventually faded. The doctors who treated my case called this a miracle. Knowing what I do now about the conscious and subconscious mind, I know exactly what happened. At this stage, so do you.

When we're children, our subconscious has not yet been contaminated and still believes in endless possibilities. I had no idea that there was a possibility I might lose my arm that day. My parents were always positive, and, luckily, my conscious mind was filled with positive thoughts. The doctors kept their comments to my parents, and my subconscious mind was never fed the idea that my arm wouldn't get better. Because I didn't know better and didn't allow negative thoughts to enter into my mind, I prevailed. Everything I experienced as a child put me on the path as an adult to create the life I now live—one where I'm able to help others and give back to my community.

As I look back at several of my own major clues, they all had significant meanings. All of the dots started to align, and my purpose in life became crystal clear. I chose to take the positive from each experience (clue) and would slowly understand the greater meaning for my life.

- My arm had been severed to point me in the direction of going into the medical profession.

- That judge who made me serve community service at a local blood bank was possibly the biggest clue that I was supposed to go into the medical field.

- The anxiety and depression experienced in college was simply another reoccurring medical clue that pointed me in the direction of the medical industry.

- Multiple car accidents with many broken bones.

- Being diagnosed with abnormal dysplasia and having to undergo cryosurgery.

- After several successful years in medical sales, being fired was God's favor in my life that pointed me into the direction of starting my own business. Remember, I didn't have the complete confidence in myself at that stage of my own journey to leave a high six-figure job and start my own business.

- My choice to sue my employer would become a major clue that solidified my faith in God.

God created each of us for an extraordinary purpose. You were created for greatness and were meant to excel. You have all of the tools you need to fulfill your destiny. You are the builder of your own life, captain of your own vessel, and you have the tools to build an incredible life. You are holding in your hands the keys to the treasure and are about to create whatever story for your life that you can envision. You can clearly see the bigger picture and now understand that you are the hero of your own story.

Whether you've been living in stage 1 of the Hero's Journey, the ordinary world, or stage 3, refusal of the call, you are now awake and recognize the clues you hadn't been able to see before. You may have already experienced your own epiphany and understand that you can no longer live the way you have been. You're ready to move past the victim stage and say goodbye to the old you. You have taken responsibility for your future and are moving toward your calling in life.

CLUE

According to the theory of aerodynamics, it should be impossible for the bumblebee to fly. He's not supposed to be able to fly because of the size, weight, and shape of his body in relation to his wingspan. However, someone forgot to tell the bumblebee about this, and he flies! The moral of the story: never let someone tell you what you can or can't do in life.

You're the Writer, Producer, Lead, and Hero of Your Own Movie

I want you to take a moment to picture the following: You're about to watch the most amazing movie of your life. You are the producer of your own movie. You are about to create your very own story, one that is called life. You've made the conscious decision to become the hero of your own story. You know your values and goals and have strong faith. You have a tremendous sense of gratitude for everything you have in your life. You are centered and in tune with who you are, and nothing else matters. You surround yourself with people who have your best interests at heart, and you've created your own mastermind team of individuals to help you achieve your greatest dreams. You are healthy, physically fit, and have a positive outlook about the future. You make smart choices about the foods you choose to fuel your body with and have started getting involved in activities that boost your self-confidence. You are keenly aware of how you speak to yourself, and you treat yourself like you would your best friend.

You wake up every morning with your gratitude journal next to your bed, giving thanks for the amazing life that you already have. You recognize the power of gratitude and have made giving thanks a regular part of your day. You write out all of the things you're grateful for before the day gets started, and it is the last act you do before you go to bed at night. You're starting to recognize that the people and events you are grateful for are expanding in your life.

You've created a treasure map that encompasses all areas of your life—personal, career, finances, life purpose, spirituality, and health and fitness. You've put a picture of yourself in the center of the map and have surrounded it with the goals you've set for yourself. Your treasure map is hanging in a spot where you can focus on it, which you do for several minutes a day. You begin to feel a sense of excitement as you resonate with the items on your treasure map. You can feel the excitement of having accomplished what is on your treasure map, as if it is already a thing of the past.

You think like a winner does, and you've implemented various techniques to train your brain to think more positively. When something goes wrong, you're constantly looking for the good in every situation. You're starting to notice that the dreams you've been thinking about are magically showing up in your life. You're aware that the universe is responding to the thoughts you've put into it. You now know that you can create anything that you truly desire.

You're the one who is going to make your dreams come true.

You have a clear understanding of your vision and purpose and have set realistic and attainable goals for yourself. Every day you're feeling more accomplished as you achieve steps toward your bigger life vision and purpose. You're clear on your primary and secondary emotions and have written your emotional life purpose statement in big letters where you can read it aloud to yourself every day. You finally know your why!

You know exactly what your strengths, talents, and skills are and have completed the fifty life events exercise in this book (and the additional fifty events you still want to achieve). You have evaluated these events and have a better understanding of why certain events and people have magically come into your life.

You are aware of the clues that surround you. Because you are leading with your heart, you're more excited than ever and are living a life of purpose that you know is right for you.

You can see the path forward and are already taking the needed steps toward your vision and purpose. You have faith and have let go of worry, doubt, and fear because you know things are working for your best interest. You've done away with skepticism and doubt and have replaced them with a sense of purpose and certainty.

Your relationship with yourself and those around you has improved to a whole new level. You have respect for everyone and everything surrounding you. You have a deep desire to discover and live a life of purpose.

You know your purpose and wake up every day with ambition, enthusiasm, gratitude, determination, self-confidence, and a positive attitude. You are willing to do what it takes to achieve your dreams and have become aware of the people, places, and events that surround you. You start to see every adversity as a blessing in disguise and immediately look for the bigger meaning in your life. You clearly see each and every clue and understand its deeper meaning. You have become your own clue catcher and understand how to start connecting all of the clues.

You've successfully eliminated skepticism and doubt from your mind. You're not allowing any negativity into your life and refuse to lose focus of your bigger vision. Whatever circumstances you're currently going through, God already knows about them, and he is working behind the scenes to arrange whatever lies ahead in your favor. You've learned to trust in the universe and quit worrying about stuff.

You're ready to face life's battles with plenty of strength and courage to overcome every obstacle thrown your way. Somewhere in the world, your place is waiting for you. Through ambition, drive, discipline, desire, backed by an unwavering amount of faith, you will never be defeated in achieving your life purpose.

You must keep the faith in the only person who controls your destiny. You are now aware that the magic key to the golden treasure is *you*. You've possessed that key the entire time. You are the key, and you are the treasure. You are no longer looking for these items outside of yourself because you now know the secret. Once you discover this, you will have struck gold. Your journey to find the treasure has just begun because your level of awareness has changed forever. Dare to dream big, because you now possess the ability to achieve any dream you dare dream.

See you at the top.

Follow the Clues

- You are the producer of your own movie—life.

- You think like a winner does, and you've implemented various techniques to train your brain to think more positively.

- You wake up every day with ambition, enthusiasm, gratitude, determination, self-confidence, and a positive attitude. You know your purpose. You know your why!

- You are now aware that the magic key to the golden treasure is *you*. You've possessed that key the entire time. You are the key, and you are the treasure. You are no longer searching for anything on the outside.

WITH THANKS

I would like to thank each of the women who contributed their stories for this book. I couldn't have completed this book without you. You are my heroes and I am forever grateful.

I would like to personally thank The Startup Studio, Gary Conroy, and Anastasia Hall for providing the forum that allowed me to uncover my God-given personal life purpose of helping this next generation of women to uncover and live their life purpose. I appreciate your support and couldn't have done this without you and your amazing forum.

I was originally introduced to The Startup Studio through Zsa Zsa Goldstrom, who is one of the best young networkers that I've ever met. It was through her networking and subsequent introductions that this book and the ongoing program of The American Interns was made possible. Thank you, Zsa Zsa, for being one of the clues who came into my life to show me the path to my personal purpose.

Through this network, as mentioned earlier, I was blessed to work with Carly Burr and Sabrina Riback. Both young women won contests conducted at their school in 2021 and were subsequently chosen as winners for a marketing and Life Purpose contest. Carly Burr came up with the marketing theme of associating the journey of finding one's life purpose to that of a treasure hunt. Both Carly and Sabrina contributed to the editing and writing of this book. In addition, Grayson Culliford worked as an intern at our M&A firm and assisted in the editing and interviewing of candidates. Grayson subsequently returned to her high school to start up a young entrepreneurship club.

ABOUT THE AMERICAN INTERNS PROGRAM

It was during the writing of *Clues* that the American Interns program was created. This program is designed to allow students worldwide to enter an annual Life Purpose contest conducted by the author of this book. The winners will have the opportunity to win an internship and cash prizes on an ongoing annual basis.

For more information on how to enter, deadlines, and details about the prizes, go to www.TheAmericanInterns.com.

Let's meet the reasons that the American Interns program exists today.

Zsa Zsa Goldstrom

"Everything happens for a reason."

From my first conversation with Melissa, I felt an instant rapport with her. She has a rare calmness about her, with a subtle twist of horsepower, confidence, and kinetic energy! She has a favorite pragmatic quote that Melissa swears is the only one she would even possibly consider: "Everything happens for a reason." This immutable mindset has always been her North Star, allowing her to pursue ventures and innovative opportunities that most people would run from. She is driven by boundless enthusiasm to continue learning, growing, and ultimately making a positive difference in other people's lives.

When I met Melissa, I was still in high school, eager to learn as much as I could from a tech-savvy female entrepreneur. She became my mentor and adviser, educating me about the professional world and the experiences and conditions she learned to navigate along the way. It was invaluable information with amazing relevancy to projects that I have begun, and it has made a significant impact on my life. I personally have been blessed with many incredible opportunities to meet successful individuals, participate in activities, and create events that have brought groups of like-minded people together.

Recently, I had the opportunity to coauthor and publish a book on cryptocurrency, blockchain, and NFTs called *The Entrepreneur's Guide to Creating and Selling Cryptocurrency and NFTs* (available on Amazon). Committing to this rigorous eight-month project ultimately showed me how fulfilling it is to educate others and motivate them to ignite their potential. In addition to that revelation, I've had doors open for speaking engagements and enthusiasm from colleges and universities across the United States for implementing the book into their academic curriculum.

Throughout my life, I've learned about the varied definitions of success that motivated individuals strive for. Some seek riches, while others seek reputation and recognition. While these are only a few readily visible indicators of achievement that I recognize as part of my own efforts, the one that appeals to me most is guiding others to success. I am continually striving to evolve into the kind of entrepreneur and leader who feels qualified and inspired to motivate and guide others on how to achieve their goals. I am in the beginning stages of my journey, preparing myself to create a relevant and achievable platform that will allow others to fulfill their aspirations.

My book, I believe, is the first step in my mentoring journey, since it teaches aspiring entrepreneurs the relevant steps to develop their own startups in a documented approach that will provide them with the tools to succeed.

Life comes with many opportunities, intriguing people, and experiences we do not always initially accept. We must base our decisions on how they will affect our lives. My mantra is to look at life through the lens of logic and optimism. Most of all, careers do not have a permanent upward trajectory, so it is critical to take advantage of the unexpected.

Meet American Intern Season 1 Winner

Carly Burr

"She believed she could, so she did."

I vividly remember the first time that I was determined to do something. My local library was hosting a book-themed cake contest, and I took it upon myself to enter and create a Wizard of Oz themed cake. I remember dragging my mom to Michaels to get fondant, and begging her to take me to McDonald's multiple times to gather the Wizard of Oz mini dolls that were being given away in Happy Meals. As I collected the ingredients and planned my cake, I felt a fierce determination within that set my soul on fire. I'm not sure why I wanted to win so badly, especially since the prize was an apron and a wooden spoon. But, I will never forget the pride and joy that I felt when they announced that I was the 1st place winner. The rest is history.

Some eight years later, here I am, taller, more mature, and grown out of my Wizard of Oz phase, still that determined girl who won the cake contest. That victory ingrained the determination in my genes. Over the years, I've applied that trait to my love for creating, including making multi-colored string bracelets that I sold at my swim club, peppermint lip scrubs that were the biggest hit at my middle school's entrepreneurship club, and custom college tailgate t-shirts that were sold on consignment at a local boutique. Currently, I am working on a business idea in the fashion field and am eager to create something new. My love for fashion grew stronger when I worked at Bloomingdale's as a sales associate this past summer. It was thrilling to be able to help people create outfits that complimented them and made them feel confident.

I was born and raised in the small town of Upper Saddle River, New Jersey until the age of 16 when my family and I moved to Delray Beach, Florida. Having made great friends and finally settled down at my high school in New Jersey, I wasn't the happiest to have to get up and move to a whole new environment. But, once I started school and joined the dance team, I quickly made new friends and realized how much I loved Florida. I learned that I needed to accept change rather than reject it. Having found my love for entrepreneurship at a young age, I dove deeper into the subject by taking the entrepreneurship class at my new school. Having many successful leaders who spoke to our class, Melissa Butterworth stood out. When she announced the contest that she was facilitating, I immediately had the same feeling that I got when I found out about the cake contest. This time, the prize was better than the spoon; it was a paid internship, $5000, and inclusion in her upcoming book. The objective was to take her existing book outline and create an overarching theme along with coordinated chapter titles. I spent hours brainstorming ideas until a lightbulb went off in my head. I got so deep into the project that I even created a mock book cover. I guess my instincts were right, because soon I was $5000 richer, and had an amazing job. The knowledge that I gained from working with Melissa has been so valuable to me, but more importantly, I found an incredible mentor who took me under her wing and gave me so many incredible opportunities.

I am currently attending the University of Miami Herbert School of Business where I am pursuing a double major in Marketing and Management. My dream is to be the CEO of my own company. I am a strong believer that you can set your mind to absolutely anything you want to do. I've thought this way since I was a child, and will never take no for an answer; You can ask my parents, they'll have a lot to say about that. The energy that you release to the universe is exactly what you are going to get back, and if you visualize and manifest, you can do just about anything. I also cannot stress enough how important and impactful your thoughts are. As mentioned in the book, everything you say to yourself has a way of entering into your subconscious mind. Changing my personal mindset and thoughts has impacted my life for the better.

When I reflect on this incredible opportunity, I credit my eight year-old self for going the extra mile, being the only contestant who dressed up in a Dorothy costume to match their cake (pictured above). Just like Dorothy kept following the yellow brick road, I'm glad I've found my own path.

Grayson Culliford

"Every cloud has a silver lining."

Hello! My name is Grayson Culliford and I am a tenth-grade student from New York City. I currently attend a boarding school called St. Andrew's School in Delaware. Ever since I was younger, I remember being fascinated by entrepreneurship. I know, how can a seven-year-old know what entrepreneurship is? I mean I was fascinated with the idea of creating something helpful.

From kindergarten through eighth grade, I attended an all-girls Catholic school. I really grew a lot there. My elementary school and middle school emphasized creating, especially in STEM and technology, which all was super interesting to me. I remember, even in the first grade, having a blast on an assignment creating a new invention of any kind. Especially at a young age, I always enjoyed those types of projects and having freedom to create new and fun inventions.

When I went into the ninth grade, I was ready for a change of environment. I loved the excitement of meeting new people and experiencing a new place. With my parents being divorced, I also wanted to be in a place that felt free of all the back and forth. Ninth grade, to be honest, was quite a blur with COVID, and I remember feeling so overwhelmed with it all.

When I met Melissa Butterworth through my mom, I remember loving talking with her. My mom had been close friends with her for quite some time, and I was especially intrigued to hear about her work. Having always been interested in starting my own company, all these concepts and things I was hearing amazed me. Melissa being an entrepreneur and a CEO of a company really inspired me and made me truly realize that I wanted to pursue this too.

In the summer before tenth grade, I interned with Melissa, and it was such an amazing learning experience. I came along on some of the company "ride days" where I would get to immerse myself in her field of work. I also got to help organize upcoming projects and observe meetings.

All these experiences showed me how far hard work can go. Being independent, striving to be the best you can be, putting yourself first, and having empathy all play into what it means to become a better person and embrace your full potential.

My parents, both doctors, show and teach me constantly the importance of hard work. Their dedication and constant care for their patients is so inspiring to see. With hard work and commitment in your life comes adversity too. It is sometimes not easy, but, in the end, everything happens for a reason. Even though I am young and still figuring out my true life purpose, I know that confidence, hard work, and perseverance go a long way toward striving for your goals.

Meet the First Annual Life Purpose Contest Winner

Sabrina Riback

"I believe in utopias and that I have the power to create my own."

Everyone has a different definition of utopia. Some people believe utopias don't exist or that a utopia is too good to be true. However, I believe in utopias and that I have the power to create my own.

The experiences that others might view as negative are vital to success and to building personal strength and character. I look at them through a positive lens, allowing them to have a positive impact on me. I believe there is a positive in every situation. This mindset has allowed me to thrive and to create my own version of a utopia.

My name is Sabrina Riback. I am a sixteen-year-old entrepreneur who is obsessed with chasing my dreams and creating my own version of a utopia through learning, listening, hard work, and determination.

When I was seven years old, I started to sell homemade bracelets at local marketplaces. When I was ten, I sold homemade pillows that I created on my sewing machine. My bracelets and pillows always sold very well. I watched endless YouTube tutorials and invested in different materials and sewing machines to start and grow my own pillow company. I went to marketplaces in nearby towns. After my success, I reevaluated my business plan and started donating a percentage of proceeds to charity. I named my company Pillows for a Purpose. For me, my utopia encompassed being an entrepreneur and giving back to the community. Going to these marketplaces set my soul on fire, and I knew this was what I was meant to do.

Through my entrepreneurial ventures, I became a leader. As class president my freshman, sophomore, and junior years of high school, I am continuing with my passions and helping to lead the school.

Starting a business is like a video game, and ambition is what gets you to that next level. Getting past level one is the hardest, but you'll learn from it and it will motivate you to keep going to get to level two. Once you get to level two, you'll be excited to reach the upcoming levels. Every time a new opportunity arises, I take that and use it as motivation and the needed fuel to work harder.

From a young age, I have always been overly empathetic. The ability to feel for someone else's situation has allowed me to strive to give back to those in need. My time at sleepaway camp the past eight summers has shaped me into an ambitious and outgoing leader.

One of the most amazing charities that sends underprivileged kids to camp is called Summer Camp Opportunities to Promote Education (SCOPE). I serve on the junior leadership committee. I started a SCOPE chapter at my school, and I am the founder and president. We fundraise and send underprivileged kids to various SCOPE camps. Nothing sets my soul on fire like giving back to a community that has personally impacted me. Giving back to an organization like SCOPE allows me to turn a negative situation into a positive one, not only for myself but for the community.

I am so grateful to attend a school that has The Startup Studio entrepreneurship program. While my biggest passion is fashion, I strive to give back to the community. I saw the immense problems of fast fashion and decided I wanted to get involved. I currently have a sustainable fashion blog that raises awareness of fast fashion and informs others how to shop in a more sustainable manner. Behind the scenes, I am creating a sustainable fashion platform that will make buying sustainable fashion more accessible. Through the entrepreneurship program, I am able to fuel my greatest passion every day and create a company that is a crucial aspect of the utopia I am creating.

In my entrepreneurship class, Melissa Butterworth, a mentor and successful entrepreneur, came to speak. I was blown away by her story and I asked her for a separate one-on-one Zoom meeting. Lucky for me, she agreed, and that is where our relationship began.

Melissa sponsored two contests: a book theme contest and a Life Purpose contest. After weeks of hard work and dedication, I was the first person to enter both contests. I was also the first person to be interviewed by Melissa. I won $5,000 for the Life Purpose contest. I treasure my relationship with Melissa, and I couldn't be more grateful for the impact she has had on my life. I am currently interning for her, helping her with various tasks and working very hard to ensure that I am adding value to her team and her company. I am learning valuable lessons that will strengthen my skill set.

My dream and life purpose are to be the CEO of a social entrepreneurship venture that provides benefits to the world around us. I am planning to study entrepreneurship and business administration in the future.

ABOUT THE AUTHOR

My name is Melissa Butterworth. I was born and raised on a farm in Harrisonburg, Virginia. I came from very humble beginnings. Both of my parents started off as schoolteachers in the early 1970s.

Even as a small kid, I enjoyed opening small businesses selling baked goods and lemonade in my neighborhood. I had a passion for serving others and always enjoyed talking to people. I was driven by the idea that I could help others while making an unlimited income. I had watched my mother's drive for success when she left teaching to pursue a venture with uncapped income potential. She ended up working in computer sales, which led her to meet a young man by the name of Michael Dell (that was my mother, Ellen, you read about earlier). She was in the right place at the right time and made a fortune utilizing her God-given strengths of helping others to achieve their goals.

During my last year in college at the University of North Florida, I started working closely with the university's career development center on résumé development, interview preparation, and networking techniques, and I worked with the staff to understand various career path options.

Having experienced some medical issues during both high school and college and having spent a summer of community service at a local blood bank, I discovered my passion for helping others in the medical field. I knew that I wanted to be in the medical field in some capacity and I'd always had an entrepreneurial spirit. These earlier events revealed significant clues that would become the compass toward finding my own treasure. It was as if someone was continuing to guide me along the way.

Prior to graduating (with honors and dual degrees in marketing and management), with the help of the career development center, I sent out résumés in video form to various executives at the top fifty pharmaceutical companies, expressing how I could contribute to their bottom line by increasing sales. This landed me my first dream job of selling pharmaceuticals to physicians' offices.

I spent the first twelve years of my career working my way up in the corporate world and eventually shifted from pharmaceutical sales to laboratory diagnostic sales. I quickly moved up the corporate ranks and eventually held one of the highest-level positions (executive director for the southeastern United States and Puerto Rico) over the hospital division for the largest laboratory in the world. My career was thriving, and I was at the top of my game.

During my thirteenth year in the corporate world, having just returned from President's Club (a prestigious club awarded annually to the top producers of the company), I was fired. I was devastated but had learned early on that every traumatic event or divine intervention (depending on how you view things) is simply a higher power redirecting our path. This was simply another clue along my own journey.

I had reached a major turning point in my career and had several options to consider. I was offered a job by the competitor, similar to the one I had held. But I intuitively knew that I was destined for something much greater and seized the opportunity to form my own company, Advanced Strategic Partners. My intuition would serve as another clue that shaped my destiny.

Today, fifteen years later, I am the cofounder, managing director, and president of Advanced Strategic Partners (advancedstrategicpartners.com). Advanced Strategic Partners is an M&A firm focused on laboratory diagnostics. I have twenty-six years of experience specific to the laboratory industry. The last thirteen years have been spent in the merger and acquisitions sector, having completed over $1.8 billion in clinical, anatomical, molecular, and hospital outreach laboratory transactions during my career.

In addition to my M&A expertise, I have spent the last decade advising molecular laboratories on new business development initiatives. I am the author of *The End Game: The Laboratory Owner's Exit Strategy* (available on Amazon).

In 2021, I became a global ambassador for the Learn to Start Institute, powered by The Startup Studio. This program creates a forum for students to take their business ideas to various entrepreneurs who provide feedback and enable them to propel their dreams into a reality.

My biggest advice to up-and-coming entrepreneurs is to look for an internship in the area that you're interested in pursuing. Find someone who has already achieved what you wish to achieve, ask them for the opportunity, and do everything you can to make their life easier by providing exceptional work for them.

Get an education and spend at least two years in the corporate world. Once you have this experience, *go for it*. Make sure you have a firm business plan and money to cover living expenses for the next year—then come up with a solution for a niche problem in the marketplace. Do your research before taking the plunge and have your plan in place. Be positive, have gratitude, and never ever give up on your dreams.

Made in the USA
Columbia, SC
25 January 2023

10277932R00143